W9-DFC-617

Through the Year in
Year in

THE MIDDLE EAST
Taqui Altounyan

Batsford Academic and Educational Ltd *London*

Acknowledgments

The Author and Publishers would like to thank the following for their kind permission to reproduce copyright illustrations: Michael Adams, page 25 (bottom); Miss E. Crowfoot, page 31; DAS Photo (James Stuart Simson), pages 7 (right), 35, 43; I.G. Dunn, page 32; Middle East Photographic Archive, pages 11 (bottom) (S. Graham-Brown), 40 (A. Duncan), 42 (right) (JVB); Christine Osborne, frontispiece, pages 7 (left), 8, 9, 11 (top), 12, 15, 16, 18, 21, 23, 24, 25 (top), 27, 28, 30, 33, 34, 36, 37, 38, 42 (left), 45, 46, 47, 49, 51, 52, 54, 55, 56, 58, 60, 62, 63, 64, 65, 66, 68; the Syrian Embassy, page 6. The map on page 5 was drawn by Rudolph Britto.

Typeset by Tek-art Ltd, London SE20
and printed in Great Britain by
R.J. Acford Ltd
Chichester, Sussex
for the publishers
Batsford Academic and Educational Ltd,
an imprint of B.T. Batsford Ltd,
4 Fitzhardinge Street
London W1H 0AH

ISBN 0 7134 4075 9

c /
+
915, 6
ALT
7 - 83

Frontispiece   Ancient and modern, Amman, Jordan. Reading the news on a Roman column.

Contents

Too much History

The "blinding light of too much history" is how one desperate Middle East writer describes it. For many thousands of years this has been the most important patch of land on earth — except perhaps for China. When the Western world was only just recovering from the last Ice Age, the Middle East was beginning to feel the first faint ripples of a great change. In the end, this was to affect the whole world, but it happened earliest and with most effect in the Middle East.

There was a quickening in the pace of the old life which had been led by small bands of hunters and gatherers for up to half a million years. For the first time, man began to influence his surroundings to his own advantage, to alter natural systems, and the most important thing was that, by so doing, he increased food production. How agriculture actually started is not really understood, but the curved sickles which have been found in the Middle East, made of deer horn, with blades of flint not very different in shape from the iron implement we have been using since the Iron Age, are undeniable evidence: tests on the antler bone give a date of at least 8000 B.C. The edges of the flint blades, stuck in with bitumen, still have an indelible "silicone gloss" like a permanent French polish — proof that they have been used to cut wheat and barley stalks.

Agriculture started with the domestication of plants and animals, which means they became completely dependent on man for survival. In the case of grain, certain forms of wild grasses which grew in the mountains nearby were chosen for harvesting because they were the most suitable for food. In the Middle East it was wheat and barley and these spread west to Europe and east to India. Wild animals became domesticated in the same random way: sheep, goats, cattle came to be herded near to permanent settlements, and they became domesticated or dependent on man because isolated from their wild relations. Evidence of this is in bones of a goat with arthritis, who grew old in the security of the home farm. He would never have survived so long in the wilds.

The crucial factor in this is that there should be a climate where wild wheat and barley will grow naturally: a rainfall of at least 300 mm per year is essential. (This is half the annual rainfall in South-East England.) This climate occurs in what used to be called "the Fertile Crescent" — a crescent of mountains starting at the head of the Persian Gulf, arching round the foothills of the Taurus in Anatolia and sending an arm down the east coast of the Mediterranean to the Dead Sea mountains of Moab. The Syrian Desert, part of which makes up Iraq, laps the inner edges of the crescent. The term Middle East could be taken to mean Egypt as well, but for this book, we will look only at the wedge of country under the influence of the rains of the Fertile Crescent.

All the first villages were in or very near the vital rainfall area. The most famous was Jericho, on the western shore of the Dead Sea. It was not far from the mountain ranges where wheat and barley grew wild, and it also had the advantage of a very abundant spring. At a time when the inhabitants of Britain were living in caves and rock shelters, Jericho was almost a town, with a deep rock-cut defence ditch and a round stone tower and about three thousand inhabitants. Pottery had not yet been discovered, and so wood and skins were used

4

For this book, the Middle East is the wedge of country affected by the rains of the Fertile Crescent. But hardly any two people agree as to what countries make up the Middle East. The name was invented during the Second World War to describe the area commanded by the British Army, with its headquarters in Cairo. Before the war it had been called the "Near East" or "The Levant", and consisted of Syria, Lebanon, Palestine, Turkey, Iraq and Egypt. A large part of Palestine became Israel in 1948. In 1939 a new term had to be found to exclude Turkey which had "gone neutral". Egypt is left out in this book because it is not part of the same geographical system; it depends on the Nile and the mountains to the east for its climate, not on the Zagros mountains and the Euphrates.

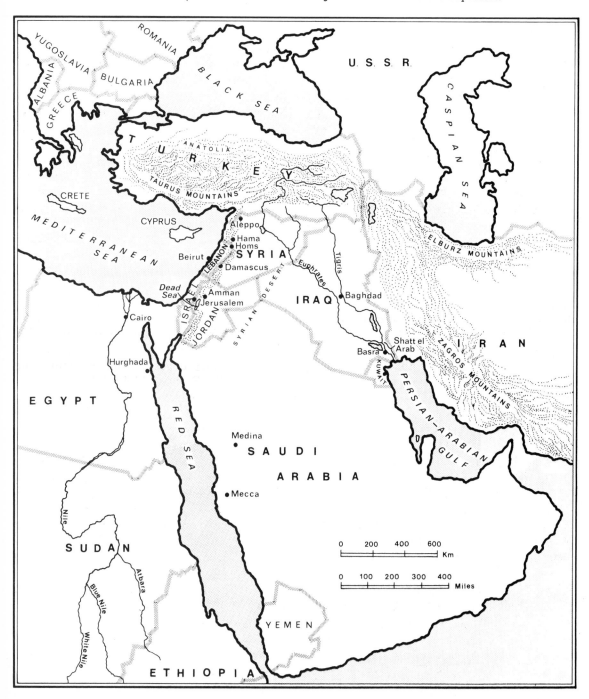

Farming near Aleppo, Syria, 1979.

Harvesting the modern way in northern Syria.

Excavating a Bronze Age tell by Lake Al-Assad, northern Syria.

and there were some very finely ground stone bowls. Besides the sickles, signs have been found of elaborate burials: most spectacular of all were skulls in which the lost flesh had been replaced with plaster, with cowrie shells for the eyes. Obsidian tools have also been discovered, which could only have come from Anatolia, many miles to the north.

As effective methods of irrigation were developed, life became possible outside the rainfall areas. First, simple trenches diverted wandering streams into neighbouring fields, but as time went on, great rivers such as the Tigris and the Euphrates which flow through otherwise desert lands had a network of complicated irrigation channels built round them. The competing needs for water of the growing and varied population meant that more and more careful organization and rationing were necessary. Greater food production led to the first "population explosion" in history and to the first towns and the first civil-service-type "admin.", as we can see from the countless clay tablets of records unearthed from towns like Babylon and Nineveh. All this happened more than six thousand years earlier than Domesday Book.

Just as important as the climate was religion. It was the link between the common people and the government and the brake which kept everything under control.

(It is still more or less so in Britain today, with the monarchy very close to the Church. It would shock the nation if Royal Weddings took place in registry offices!) In the first towns, the temple owned all the wealth and all the power and formed the apex of a very solid pyramid of organization.

The Middle East is dotted up and down the country with mounds or "tells", as they are called in Arabic. These are evidence of the country's long history and are the result of thousands of years of building and destruction on the same site. Slice through any of them and there you have it all, like layers of a chocolate cake!

These "thousands of years" will perhaps mean more to us if we reflect that it is only in the last two thousand years that technology has developed through steam power and atomic energy to space shuttles and man's first landing on the moon.

Climate, geography and religion have combined to make the Middle East a place where things have happened which are still affecting the Western world today. The wheel was invented here, and writing, and there is the massively important fact that three religions were founded in the Middle East. That is why we find religion and race so tightly bound together and so vitally important in today's daily life.

7

January

The Birth of Mohammed

Nowadays the Prophet Mohammed's birthday comes in the winter months and sometimes coincides with Christmas and the New Year in the Western world. It is celebrated in Arab countries as a public holiday, with outdoor festivities and fairs. Pink sugar dolls are sold in the streets, which seem to have as much to do with the actual event of Mohammed's birth as Father Christmas and plum pudding with the birth of Christ.

Mohammed's birthday is more a religious celebration than a family one and a lot of it takes place in the mosques. But sometimes, in the homes, elderly women will gather round and read stories about Mohammed's parents' life and doings. These are folk tales and not part of the Khoran or the Hadith. At the end, when the vital point in the story has been reached and Mohammed is born, everyone stands up and sugared almonds are handed round in special packets tied with ribbons.

In the Middle East birthdays are not important and are rarely celebrated. People are usually vague about the actual date of their birth. Parents remember the time of year when their children were born by events like a fall of snow or a specially good or bad harvest — or a war.

One complication about life in the Middle East is calendars. So many different ones are constantly in use — for business, for praying, according to whether you are Jewish, Christian or Muslim — though these days, in towns, for business and social occasions, it is more convenient to agree.

Clearing snow in front of a modern mosque in ▷
Amman, Jordan.

Three Religions

The three important religions of the Western world started in the Middle East. The Jews, the Christians and the Muslims all look upon this particular patch of earth as most holy because it inspired their three separate faiths.

Abraham, Jesus and Mohammed were all born and brought up at the edge of deserts and, as they grew up, they each felt the need to withdraw there for a time to work out the message which God was urging them to give to the world. They needed to be alone and the desert was the handiest place in which to find solitude. In the West, where deserts are few, thinkers have sought solitude in the mountains, in monasteries or on the sea. But European travellers, over the centuries, have also been specially drawn to deserts and, as they swayed over endless miles, on their

camels, some of them came to realize how the desert light and the stark landscape could encourage abstract thought which could very well be religious. In recent times the most famous of these travellers was T.E. Lawrence — Lawrence of Arabia.

In his book, *The Seven Pillars of Wisdom*, Lawrence told this story, to show the heightened aesthetic senses of his companions in the desert:

we had ridden far out over the rolling plains of North Syria to a ruin of the Roman period which the Arabs believed was a desert palace; the clay was said to have been kneaded for greater richness

Dung cakes dried in the sun are stored in these beehive-like mounds to be used as fuel. In North Syria whole villages are of houses this shape.

THE ISLAMIC CALENDAR

As the Middle East is officially Muslim, the Islamic calendar is the official one. The Western year 1980 C.E. (Christian Era) is year 1400 Hijjra on the Islamic calendar, which counts the years from the year Mohammed made his journey or "Hijjra" from Mecca to Medina, where he was able to found his new religion. The year 622 A.D. was year one of the Islamic or Hijjra calendar.

The Muslim year is lunar : each month begins on the evening that the new crescent moon is seen. But twelve lunar months only amount to 354 days — about eleven and a quarter days short of the solar year. In pre-Islamic times seven months were added over a period of nine years, to keep even with the solar calendar, which was important because of agriculture. It was convenient, if not essential, to know when crops should be planted. But Mohammed banned this : the lunar calendar was the only one. It is not really known why he did this, but in Southern Arabia where he was born there was not much farming and journeys were most often made at night. The desert Arab thinks of the moon as a friend, and the sun as his enemy.

The effect of following lunar months is that each year religious festivals fall eleven days earlier than the year before. Just at present, the slipping Muslim calendar co-incides with the Western calendar.

(An extra day is put into the year, to make 355, eleven times every thirty years.)

The months on the Islamic calendar are:

Safar	Sha'aban
Rabi al Awwal	Ramadan
Rabi al Akhir	Shawwal
Jumada al Awal	Dhu al Qa'adah
Jumada al Akhir	Dhu al Hijja
Rajab	Muharram

The meanings of these names are obscure. "Rabi al Awwal" means "the first rains" and "Rabi al Akhir" means "the last rains" — in other words, spring. "Ramadan" means "summer heat" in Arabic.

not with water but with the precious essential oils of flowers: my guides sniffing the air like dogs led me from room to crumbling room saying "this is jasmine, this violet, this rose". At last they came to an open window with a wide view over the Euphrates flowing below and the land rolling towards Iraq beyond, and there "drank with open mouths the effortless empty eddyless wind of the desert throbbing past. That slow breath had been born somewhere beyond the distant Euphrates and had dragged its way across many days and nights of dead grass to its first obstacle — the man made walls of our broken palace . . . 'this' they told me 'is the best; It has no taste.'

Gertrude Bell, a friend of Lawrence, who knew Arabs and the desert as well if not better than he did, described getting up in the cool of the morning as "waking in the heart of an opal". And when her party was in the saddle again, ready for the day's journey,

the glorious cold air intoxicated every sense and set the blood throbbing — to my mind the saying about the Bay of Naples should run differently 'see the desert on a fine morning and die — if you can.' Even the stolid mules felt the breath of it and raced across the spongey ground till their packs swung around and brought them down.

LAWRENCE OF ARABIA

Thomas Edward Lawrence ("T.E." to his friends, "Ned" to his family) is known to the world as Lawrence of Arabia (1888-1935). He was born in North Wales, the second of a family of five sons. His father, Robert Chapman (who assumed the name Lawrence), was the younger son of an Anglo-Irish landowning family. His mother, Sarah Maden, was the daughter of a Sunderland engineer, brought up in Scotland.

Lawrence was slightly but strongly built. He broke his leg as a teenager and that stopped him growing. Having learnt to read at the very early age of four, from hearing his elder brother being taught, he learnt Latin at six and for the rest of his life won scholarships at school and university. At Oxford he became interested in Crusaders and their castles and in his holidays toured Europe on his pushbike, visiting Crusader sites. The same interest took him to Palestine and Syria, where he wandered about on foot, with hardly any luggage — which was not something young Europeans often did then. Sir Leonard Woolley, the famous archaeologist, gave him a job after Oxford on one of his digs in Syria — "the best life I ever lived" Lawrence called it afterwards. He learnt Arabic and the habit of eating Arab food and wearing Arab clothes.

During the First World War he was in the intelligence service for the campaign in which the British and the Arabs fought the Turks, who were on the German side. He met the Grand Sherif of Mecca and became a bosom friend and confidant of his third son, Feisal. He describes the whole campaign in his book The Seven Pillars of Wisdom. The capture of Damascus by the British and the Arabs combined was the high spot in Lawrence's activities. He did his best at the subsequent Peace Conference to further the Arab cause. But Syria was made a French Mandate and Feisal was turned out. Though Feisal became King of Iraq and his brother Abdullah King of Transjordan, this was not the complete independence from the West that they had hoped for.

Lawrence hid from the limelight in the RAF, happily designing speedboats. He was retired at forty-six, but could not settle or enjoy his unaccustomed leisure in his cottage, Clouds Hill. One May morning he was killed, on his high-speed motor-bike, swerving while trying to avoid two boys riding abreast.

GERTRUDE BELL

Gertrude Bell (1868-1926) came to Iraq before the First World War and eventually became Oriental Secretary to the British Administration for the Mandate of Iraq set up after the expulsion of the Turks in 1917. She was a scholar, writer, linguist and, above all, an intrepid traveller who performed amazing journeys on camel-back across the Arabian desert and on horseback from Jerusalem to Aleppo, taking about three months, as described in her book *The Desert and the Sown*. Her books and her letters show an intense appreciation of Arabs and their country. Her undistinguished grave is in the Christian cemetery in Baghdad.

Rocky desert in the al-Hasma region of southern Jordan. Deserts are not always sand.

The souq, old Jerusalem.

Jerusalem

Jerusalem is set on a bare rocky hill with a dizzy view over the edge of the Syrian desert. As Christians have compared Jerusalem to heaven and it is often called "the Golden", one almost imagines everything there to be of gold. This is, of course, not so, but the dry, pine-scented air and the light over the city, which is so dazzling and beautiful, make it easy to imagine Jerusalem being the inspiration of religions.

To do ordinary things, like getting shoes mended, at a shop near one of the stations of the Cross, is something one never takes for granted. Picnics in the Garden of Gethsemane, or expeditions to the top of the Tower of the Ascension of the Russian

Tourists at the spot where Christ preached by the Dead Sea.

Convent, on Mount Scopus, to see the sun rise over the Dead Sea and the mountains of Moab on Ascension Day can never be quite

---

THE HEBREW OR JEWISH CALENDAR

The Hebrew calendar is more complicated even than the Islamic. It is solar for the year and lunar for the months. The normal year has 353-355 days in twelve lunar months; but seven times in each nineteen years an extra month of 30 days is intercalated to adjust the calendar to the solar year. New year or Rosh Hoshana (the same as in Arabic Ras el Sana, meaning head of the year) usually falls in September, but the day varies considerably. The Hebrew calendar is only used to calculate the dates of the Jewish religious festivals. The months are:

Tishri	Nisan
Marcheshvan	Iyyar
Kislev	Sivan
Tebeth	Tammus
Shebat	Ab
Adar	Ellul

THE GREGORIAN CALENDAR

In most Arab countries the Islamic calendar is used side by side with the Gregorian calendar, for official purposes. The months are:

January	Kanoon al Tani
February	Shabat
March	Adhar
April	Nizan
May	Mayiss or Ayar
June	Haziran
July	Tamus
August	Ab
September	Ayul
October	Tshrine al Awal
November	Tshrine al Tani
December	Kanoon al awal

like any other outing — however long you live in Jerusalem. It is the same for Jews and Muslims as well as Christians. The mystical atmosphere is not to be denied. An elderly lady who found herself in Jerusalem for many years because of the Second World War, which prevented her from leaving, and who was not a believer in any of the three religions, wrote:

On a still hot day when the Mountains of Moab are reflected in the Dead Sea and the whole country shimmers with heat haze everything seems to fall away out of sight below the horizon till the hills of Bethlehem bring you up to sanity and safety again. This is an uncanny country. No wonder it produced a few queer people.

February

Damascus

Pink almond blossom — sudden shocking colour in the sea of silver grey evergreen olive trees — tells us that spring is on the way, before any leaves are on the trees, and while days are still cold.

In the famous gardens or orchards which ring Damascus, all kinds of fruit trees are mixed together with olive and poplar and walnut trees, and the spare earth between is planted with kitchen gardens and with vines, all irrigated, as of old, by runnels from neighbouring streams. Among this conglomeration are square houses built round a courtyard, with flat roofs and sometimes pools. This is the centre of the estate, where the gardener-farmer lives all the year round and his master,

Mud houses and almond blossom.

the landowner, may come at weekends or during the hot days of summer. Part of the house may be a stables, with a cow and calves and a few chickens running about, giving the gardens an undefined farm-like air. All this makes up the famous Ghuta, which rings Damascus, pushing back the desert, and which over the centuries has made the city seem an earthly paradise to the many thousands who live in drier parts. (It is said that Mohammed refused to visit the city, not wishing to anticipate the joys of Paradise.)

It is sad that, today, this paradise is being gradually eaten into by roads which each year encroach a little more on the thousands of little gardens. But great circular painted boxes of crystallized fruits are surviving reminders of the lush orchards and the ancient skill of the sweet-makers. The sugary fruits are arranged like jewels in their boxes, some of which are large enough to be trundled along like a wheel by a small child. Almost always, in the centre, is a round of purple pistachio nuts stuck together with sugar.

Saladin and the Crusades

The Islamic calendar this month remembers the death of Saladin, or Salah ud Din, nearly eight hundred years ago, at the age of fifty-six. Saladin was the driving force and the inspiration of the Arab resistance to the Crusades. He was a man of immense energy and a skilful general, and his broadness of vision, which made him work for the unity of the Arabs, was not common in those self-seeking days. Nor was his altruism : at times he was so kind that his enemies spread the story that he must have had an English mother.

THE CRUSADES

The Crusades started in about 1000 A.D., a hundred years after the peak of Arab conquest of the West. There were three waves of Crusades, spread over about two hundred years. It all began in response to the Pope's call for a great armed pilgrimage to expel the Muslims from Palestine — more especially from Jerusalem, the "cradle of Christianity". He promised that all who died on a Crusade, however bad their lives had been before, would go straight to Heaven.

The First Crusade was successful: the Crusaders captured Jerusalem from the Arab armies, as well as other important towns in Palestine. They set up a number of small states of which the most important was "the Latin kingdom of Jerusalem" under King Baldwin. Two orders of Knights were founded, which still mean something today: the Knights Templars and the Knights Hospitallers (who originally ran a hospital in Jerusalem). They were, in effect, a sort of military monks who took vows of poverty, chastity and obedience. The Knights Templars wore a tunic over their armour with a large red cross sewn on it; for the Hospitallers it was a white cross on black. This, of course, made them easily distinguishable in battle, especially on horseback. Each knight was in command of ten men who had been recruited from their estates back home. The numbers involved were small by today's standards.

At first, a knight in full armour, on a horse much larger than the Arab steeds, was as invincible as a tank. But after the first shock, the Arabs learnt to make full use of their vastly superior numbers and the ease with which they could manoeuvre their wiry little steeds in land which they knew well. Jerusalem was retaken from the Crusaders by Saladin, who also won back most of the other lands they had conquered. Before long even the last Crusader strongholds on the coast fell, and the last boatloads of dispirited Crusaders left for the West.

But, in a very general way, the conflict is still going on today. Though Saladin had retaken Jerusalem, he had not wiped out all Western influence there — the Christian powers had managed to hang on to enough to give them a say in who should look after their Holy Places in Jerusalem and Bethlehem. In the nineteenth century, the Crimean War against the Ottoman Turks, who were rulers of all the Middle East, was a successful effort by the West to keep its influence. After the First World War, Palestine and Syria, which made up a large part of the Middle East, were given to Britain and France to look after, as mandates, and that too may perhaps be seen as a result of the "long afterswell" of the Crusades, as one historian has put it. The conflict between the Western world and the Islamic East has led the area to be called "the most vexed region of history".

"Kerak of the Knights".

The battles of the Crusades were often a chivalrous conflict between individuals; and the super-stars of these duels were Saladin and the Crusader King, Richard Coeur de Lion. The story goes that once, when the Crusader had been thrown from his horse, Saladin stopped the action while he sent over a fresh mount. Though he sometimes had all the garrison of a defeated fortress massacred, as was the custom, at other times he unexpectedly spared them, and he is reported to have broken down in tears after the capture of Jerusalem, at the sight of the women mourning over their dead knights. In *The Talisman* by Sir Walter Scott, which has been made into a television serial, Richard and Saladin display their swordsmanship, one by splitting an iron block by sheer force and the other by severing a falling veil with a flick of his curved scimitar. While historians seem to go out of their way to recount the most horrible instances of cruelty in order to show the power of their heroes, in the case of Saladin his actual humane personality has survived as well as his toughness.

Saladin is buried in Damascus and an inscription on his tomb thanks him for liberating Jerusalem from the "blemish of the unbelievers". His epitaph reads: "Oh God receive this soul and open to him the doors of paradise; the last conquest for which he hoped". Legend says that he died so poor that his friends were obliged to borrow money to bury him decently. As he lay dying, he summoned his standard bearer and told him: "You who carried my banner in the wars will now carry it in my death — let it be a vile rag set upon a lance." As the simple procession struggled through the narrow streets, the crowd was heard to remark: "Lo, at his death the King of the East could take nothing but this rag only."

Crusader Castles

The greatest legacy of the Crusaders in Syria are the castles which are positioned up and down the country. Communication between them was by carrier pigeons, an art learnt from the Muslims. Lawrence of Arabia described "Kerak of the Knights" as "perhaps the most admirable castle in the world". Another much more recent traveller, Robin Fedden, told how its outer wall, 24 metres thick, earned it the name of "the mountain" with the "astonished Muslims". For a hundred and fifty years without a break, the Crusaders lived inside the castle. The full garrison was two thousand strong. Life continued inside the walls from generation to generation: the babble of Medieval French was heard in guard room and chapel.

Saladin never managed to take the castle of Kerak, but he did manage to take Sayhoun "after a mere seventy years of (Crusader) occupation". Today the Syrians call Sayhoun "Saladin's Castle". It has one feature which is a monument to the amazing energy and determination of the Crusaders: a tremendous channel 33 metres deep, cut out of the solid rock, which separates the ridge on which the castle stands from the rest of the hill, making it an island in the air. In the middle of the channel, a pinnacle of rock has been left on its own to form the base for a drawbridge. In the days before dynamite every inch of that cutting must have been achieved somehow with hammer and chisel!

15

March

Spring

At present, the Islamic month of "Rabi al Akhir", meaning "last rains", coincides with March, and this month does see the last of the rains and the height of spring. It is interesting that in the 1980s the year has come round to what it was in 622 A.D., when Mohammed fixed the calendar.

In Northern Iraq this bursting out period of sun and flowers is called "Nawruz" which is the Persian word for spring.

All of a sudden, the fields and plains, groves and valleys run with colour. Every girl and woman erupts into the landscape in clothes that seem to be stitched from the brightest rainbow you can imagine. (Gavin Young, *Iraq*, Collins, 1980)

Cooking fish by the Tigris river, in Iraq, to celebrate Nawruz.

In Syria, the people of the towns of Aleppo and Hama celebrate a spring festival. Pitching their tents in the flowering desert, they eat tremendous meals at which sheep are roasted whole, and spend the days and nights in song, music and dancing. It is, for many of them, to go back, in a comfortable and idyllic form, to the life of their ancestors as wandering Bedouin. But townspeople of all faiths who happen to own land near the cities, in the form of fields, like to pitch tents among the green corn for a week or two, so that their horses and their families can enjoy the spring.

Tourists in the Middle East

The spring — and the autumn — are the favourite times for tourists. In spring pilgrims come to celebrate the Christian festival

Spring in Amman, Jordan — bright costumes and local dancing.

16

LEBANON

Lebanon is an enormous upfold of rock parallel to the coast, with a very narrow coastal strip. Between two folds of mountain is the Bekaa plain in which rise two rivers: the Orontese, which flows north and through Turkey before reaching the sea after many windings, and the Litani, which flows south and suddenly makes a bend towards the Mediterranean, not far from the border with Israel. An unusual feature, which makes Lebanon different from Syria and Israel, is that in the rocky upfold is a layer of non-porous rock, through which rain cannot penetrate, so that the hills are covered with unexpected springs. Added to this, the highest mountain Sannin, is 9,000 feet high and covered with snow from December to May, giving the country its name. "Leban" means "white" in Aramaic. Another odd thing about Lebanon is that it has a higher rainfall than Manchester, but less than half the number of rainy days. Great storms occur and the rain reaches almost monsoon fierceness while it lasts. In summer the humidity is so high that you feel as though you are trying to breathe through a wet felt horse blanket.

After the First World War, when the Middle East was divided up into Mandates, the French created the "State of the Greater Lebanon", a new republic about the size of Wales. The state was founded on a balance between different religious communities. The President was always a Christian and the Prime Minister a Muslim. The cabinet posts were held by representatives of the various religions on a proportional basis. So delicate is the balance that it is still considered dangerous to take a census and there has not been one since 1932. It is thought that the Muslims form 60% of the population because of a higher birth and a lower emigration rate. The Maronite Catholics are the largest single Christian community but there are also large communities of Greeks and Armenians. But most foreigners and foreign businesses have now left the country — and hundreds of thousands of skilled and semi-skilled workers who were the backbone of Lebanese economy and private enterprise — mainly for Saudi Arabia. Also, the damage to industry has put thousands of those who remain out of work — food processing, yarn spinning and textiles mainly. Lebanon has never had much oil, but it is the terminus of two of the most important pipelines and at each terminus there is a refinery.

Intercommunal strife is never far from the surface. As in the other Middle East countries, the presence of Israel just across the border and of a large number of Palestinians inside Lebanon, add to the tension. In 1975 an attack was made by Palestinians on some Christians in a bus, which led to the Christians killing the passengers of the bus who were mainly Palestinians. (Although, in the main, Palestinians tend to be Muslim, this is not by any means always the case. In the case of the war with Israel, Muslims and Christians alike can fight in the Palestine Liberation Organization.) Things escalated, so that Syria launched full-scale intervention. In spite of all that the Joint Arab Peace-keeping Force and United Nations Forces could do, Beirut, the Lebanese capital, was soon shot to bits and the economy and way of life were in ruins.

In 1979 Mahor Haddad, a right-wing Lebanese Christian Army Officer, proclaimed "independent free Lebanon" — i.e. 700 square miles of territory next to the Israeli border. Encouraged by Israel, he continued to reign in what came to be known as "Haddadland". In the face of all this, President Sarkis continued to issue rather pathetic messages to what he still called his "nation", affirming his belief in the unity of the land, his total opposition to mini-states and militias, his allegiance to parliamentary democracy, and more important, stating his belief that Lebanon was above all an Arab country and therefore that he rejected the Camp David Agreement and supported a Palestinian State, co-operation with Syria and support for the United Nations Forces in South Lebanon. For Lebanon, tolerance and compromise between different communities is a matter of survival.

In June 1982 the Israelis invaded Lebanon with the stated aim of wiping out the P.L.O., which had made its headquarters in the country. Their excuse was the attempt on the life of their ambassador in London. In the full-scale attack by land, sea and air, thousands of civilians of all nationalities were killed, as well as Palestinians, and, in a very short time, the ones who remained were held in a ring of steel in Beirut. All food was stopped and even water and electricity supplies cut off — until international protests were made. Negotiations went on for weeks and when, finally, the Palestinian fighters had to leave, they had managed to save some of their honour; the violence of their enemy had won them new sympathy all over the world. For the first time, dissenting voices were heard, even inside Israel — while the fighting was going on.

of Easter. There are so many reasons for visiting the Middle East that it is impossible to list tourist attractions without writing a book. The Lebanon used to be the playground. It had all the advantages for holiday-makers, who could, for instance, ski in the mornings and bathe in a not too cold sea later in the day. With the mountains close to the sea, there was always some pleasant place to go to all through the year. Also, the easy-going Mediterranean nature of the Lebanese (who, some say, sat about in pyjamas all day) added to the pleasantly relaxed holiday mood and so attracted tourists from the West, as well as from other less relaxed Arab countries such as Saudi Arabia. But the bitter fighting has destroyed many of the famous hotels, and even the toughest international holiday-makers are frightened away. No Middle East government wants foreigners to get mixed up in their fighting. Strangers are the first to be whisked away if trouble seems imminent.

Jordan is the country where most tourists are seen these days, as it is generally felt to be more "safe" than other countries of the Middle East. Also, it is nearest to the great holy places now in Israel — Jerusalem, above all. Visitors to Jordan doubled between 1977 and 1978, reaching 2½ million in that year. There are no comparable figures for Iraq, which had half a million in 1977, and, apparently, none since. Lebanon had over 3 million before fighting broke out. Syria's tourists dropped a little during the same years, though the number has never been high. Israel counted about 1 million tourists in 1978 and the figure has been increasing steadily since 1977, when the Treaty with Egypt may have accounted for some of the new visitors. Egypt's figures show that the numbers of Arab tourists to Egypt fell a little after 1977. Numbers of Americans increased a great deal, and numbers of "Europeans" and "others" quite a lot. Germans are by far the most usual tourists in the Middle East — as in the rest of the world. Groups from the Far East can be seen sitting

Tourists at Hurghada, Egypt, on the Red Sea.

silently in the lounge of the Hotel Omayad in Damascus. Though there are lone travellers from England, France and Italy, and some groups travelling for special educational purposes, they are not so many now. A stranger is noticed at once in the crowded cities of Syria and Iraq. He always attracts a small convoy of little boys and young men diligently keeping pace and offering advice and things for sale with varying degrees of tact. Though never as bad as in Egypt, the "locals" can be a nuisance and seem to regard strangers as free shows — especially women. Many a photographer has had his carefully thought-out picture spoilt at the last moment by a well-timed hand or grinning face thrust in front of the lens. But there is not so much of this in Jordan and it

18

JORDAN

"A rose red city half as old as time" — this is how a poet in the nineteenth century described Petra in Jordan. Jordan's only claim to world-wide fame, Petra was carved out of a rocky rift valley of stone which was rose red and all other colours of the rainbow in about the third century A.D. by the Nabateans. The elaborate fronts of the carved palaces, imitating Greek temples, and the fine pottery scattered all over the place show that the Nabateans must have been a civilized race, but little is known of them now.

Amman, the modern capital of Jordan, is in a rift valley too. A few years ago it was a desert town, its only street crowded with Bedouin and a perfect Roman amphitheatre dominating the scene. There did not seem to be any room for expansion in the huddle of primitive houses. Today the scene is quite different.

The state of Transjordan was created, under British auspices, in 1921, after the First World War, on the East Bank of the river Jordan, as a consolation prize for the Emir Abdullah, member of the Hashemite family, who was directly descended from Mohammed. His brother was King Feisal, who had fought with Lawrence of Arabia against the Turks. During the first Arab-Israeli war of 1948-49 Abdullah annexed the West Bank of Jordan — the part of Palestine remaining in Arab hands after the partition — to form the Hashemite Kingdom of Jordan. Abdullah was assassinated by a Palestinian, and a year later his mentally unbalanced son handed over to his son, then only seventeen, the British-educated Hussein. That was in 1950 and few expected the little kingdom to last, but King Hussein is gaining a reputation for being the longest-surviving Middle East monarch.

He has certainly had problems. Since he came to the throne, his country has been turned upside down twice by two wars in the space of twenty years. The problem of absorbing refugees is worse than in any other country today. Though most of these were in camps and fed and looked after by the United Nations, the fact remained that Palestinians, mainly traders and professional men, had little in common with the inhabitants who were Bedouin engaged in herding their flocks and wandering about the vast areas of desert. In the 1967 war the West Bank went back to the Israelis. This meant a loss of 80% of cereal and fruit and vegetable growing land, the dispossession of many small farmers who were suddenly deprived of the only life they had known for many generations. But the worst blow was the loss of Jerusalem and Bethlehem. As well as the emotional shock, there was the complete breakdown of the tourist trade and the consequent loss of foreign exchange. Before 1967 earnings from the tourist trade were the only important "invisible export". In 1968 this was reduced to nothing. However, in 1975 the Jordan government took the wise if painful step of allowing visitors to its country to cross over into Israel. Before this, a stamp in a passport on the same page as a visa for Israel might have landed its owner in jail. The immediate result was that the number of tourists arriving in the country increased by 79% and the income from tourism exceeded the pre-war level. Twenty-five new hotels are being built and the port of Aqaba, on the Red Sea, is about to be developed as an international tourist resort. The war in Lebanon has meant that many businesses have transferred to Amman and the city is experiencing a minor boom. The little Bedouin town has overflowed onto the surrounding barren rocky hills in a flowering of villas, gardens and swimming pools and the new life style reminds many of pre-war Lebanon.

will, of course, get better as more tourists arrive.

Easter

Christians celebrate Easter by visiting their Holy Places. Some of the churches have no chairs and so people stand packed together, breathing in the incense and the smell of garlic and sweaty bodies. Easter ceremonies begin on Good Friday night. The long service enacts all the steps of the arrest, trial, and crucifixion of Christ, leading up to the dramatic moment when Christ cries to heaven and dies, "and the veil of the temple was rent in twain". At this moment the purple hanging which has hidden the altar throughout the ceremony is drawn aside. It is almost like a Miracle Play of Medieval times in England. Easter Saturday is usually spent recovering from the vigil in church, cooking and cleaning houses. Then, on Sunday morning, early, everyone goes to church again to find the altar decorated, the candles lit and everyone full of hope and joy because "Christ is risen from the dead". "Holy is the rising of Christ" is the reply. This is the greeting for Easter morning. It is repeated in Arabic, Armenian, Russian, and many other tongues. After church, a lot of visiting street sellers do a brisk trade in coloured eggs and a special kind of spiced, slightly sweet bread only eaten at Easter.

St. Symeon Stylites

One of the earliest places Christians used to go to was the cathedral of St. Symeon Stylites who lived as early as the fourth century A.D. He was called Stylites from a Greek word meaning "pillar", because he spent more than half his life on the top of a column.

Fifty kilometres north of Aleppo is Kalaat Semaan, which means in Arabic "the castle of Symeon". It is positioned, like the Crusader castles, on a spur of rock overlooking vast sweeps of country. In Arab times it

was a castle; the defence wall round is still visible. But, about two hundred years earlier, it was world-famous for being the shrine of St. Symeon the Stylite. On the mountainous ground where, in his lifetime, his column stood, four cathedrals were built, after his death, in the shape of a cross with an open-air octagonal in the middle, out of which the top of the column protruded. This was at least four hundred years before any of the well-known European cathedrals were built.

Symeon's life as a holy man began early. At the age of sixteen he took to wearing an iron-spiked belt under his clothes, which drew blood. Then he dug a hole in the monastery ground where he was studying and buried himself up to his chin. Dug out again just before he died under the hot sun, he next walled himself up as a Lent Penance. His elders were not impressed with all this — perhaps they thought he was showing off and exaggerating. They expelled him from the monastery. Nothing daunted, he next chained himself to a rock on the top of a high mountain and from that it was only another short step to a pillar; he began with quite a low column, but it increased to 18 metres. The platform at the top was 1 metre in diameter with a low wall to prevent him falling off. As another precaution, he was bolted to the rock by an iron collar and chain, which gave him room to kneel but never to lie down. He ate once a week, never slept, and wore a sheepskin robe and cap.

Pilgrims came from all over the world, including from Britain, to stand and gaze up at him — perhaps to catch some airy word wafted down. Some imagined that they saw visions such as a bright star suspended very low over the saint's head. At last, in his sixty-ninth year, he died quietly in a praying attitude which no-one dared to interrupt for three days. When at last one of his disciples dared to climb a ladder up to him, they found his dead body "emitting a delightful odour".

After his death the place became even more famous, like an eastern Lourdes.

A whole industry grew up which flourished till the Arabs came. And Symeon was not the only saint on a pillar — a junior saint somewhere near the town of Antioch in north Syria was said to have "cut his teeth in that situation".

Quite a lot of this Middle East Lourdes can be seen today near the Saint's hill. The town of Bara is still a complete city with many of the houses standing as if built out of children's bricks — not a scrap of mortar was used in the whole complex. Once of dazzling white limestone, they have now turned grey. The roofs and upper floors which were made of wood have disappeared, of course, but the holes for the beams are still visible. The wine and olive oil presses could still be used today. Many of the doorways have crosses on them, as the inhabitants of these dead villages were very conscious of their new and exciting faith.

Pilgrims in Jerusalem

Jerusalem is the greatest magnet for pilgrimage for Christians, as it was the scene of the life and death of Jesus Christ. To kiss the earth of the Holy Land (that is, "holy" for the Christians — but the land is also "holy" for two other religions!) was the dream of Christians all over the world, though the Bible does not lay down any rules about visiting holy places. At the beginning of the twentieth century, for instance, tens of thousands of Russians poured yearly into the "Holy Land" from the furthest ends of the Russian Empire (before the Revolution) — old men and women, for the most part, who had pinched and saved all their lives.

They came on foot to the Black Sea where they took ship as deck passengers . . . . Morning and evening they gathered in prayer before an icon hanging in the cook's galley, and the sounds of their litanies went to heaven, mingled with the throb of the screw and the splash of the spray. They reached Jerusalem just before

A priest leaves the Church of the Holy Sepulchre, Jerusalem.

Christmas and stayed till after Easter that they might light their tapers at the sacred fire that breaks out from the Holy Sepulchre on the morning of the Resurrection. (From *The Desert and the Sown* by Gertrude Bell)

This Ceremony of the Holy Fire is unique in Jerusalem. Those who have seen it are unlikely ever to forget it. The Church of the

21

Holy Sepulchre, which is supposed to stand over the place where Christ was buried when he was taken down from the cross, is crammed with people, jammed up against one another like bristles in a hairbrush — each person grasping a limp wax candle. There is no room even to take a deep breath. If anyone should faint, he has to be carried out over the heads of the crowd, which will not give away an inch of hard-won ground. Up to the roof, there are people looking down from any opening where they have managed to find a place. Some are lying full-length on pieces of scaffolding. Some have been there all night. There is a smell of warm human bodies and incense, conversation mixed with chanting, an occasional miserable baby cry . . . . At last a flame shoots out from the round window in the sepulchre in the centre of the crowded octagon. The officiating priest lights his candle and soon — like fire spreading in a cornfield — everyone is shielding a flame in his hand, each candle will go out of the church to light other candles in the city, and perhaps on to other places roundabout. "Christ is Risen. Glorious is the Rising of Christ" is chanted in many languages.

April

Syrian Independence

In the First World War, fought by Britain and France ("the Allies") and later America against Turkey and Germany, it was important that the Arabs helped — or at least did not hinder — the Allies. The most powerful person for the Arabs was the Sherif of Mecca; he was thirty-seventh in descent from the Prophet Mohammed. At any time, his word could launch a "Jihad" or holy war against whichever side he chose. Britain made a pact with him to recognize and protect an independent Arab state or confederation of states after the war if he came in on their side. Feisal, one of the sons of the Sherif of Mecca, was persuaded by Lawrence of Arabia to lead his Arabs against the Turks. This was very important to Britain because it immobilized some 30,000 of the enemy. The Arab forces were mainly armed tribesmen with a core of regular troops and they carried out valuable guerilla operations, very much helping the British Expeditionary Force. But even as Lawrence was persuading Feisal that he would be rewarded by being made king of Greater Syria, he was quite aware that the British Foreign Office was making plans to carve up the country into mandates. After the war, France was given a mandate over Syria.

Despite the fact that French rule gave Syria a degree of law and order which might have made possible a change from a medieval to a more modern form of society, the Arabs were very angry and tried to stage a revolt which the French subdued by bombing Damascus — twice. For the next ten years French efforts to conclude a Franco-Syrian Treaty did not meet with much success, partly because they refused to recognize Greater Syria. The French also stuck to their old plan of "divide and "rule" and liked to keep their mandate divided up into as many small departments as possible. It was not until after the Second World War that Syria finally achieved independence.

Syrian Independence Day, 17 April, commemorates the day when the last foreign troops left the country and Syria was on its own for the first time since the beginning of the sixteenth century, when it became part of the Ottoman Empire. The day is celebrated mainly with a parade of troops in the big towns of Damascus and Aleppo. Arches are put up of intertwined flags, carpets and greenery, with portraits of the President (whoever he happens to be) prominently displayed as large blown-up photographs or hideous oil paintings. Aircraft fly overhead, some of them scattering showers of sweets. Clouds of white pigeons are let out of cages to flutter against the cloudless sky and add to the excitement. Shops and schools and offices are closed by public edict, and the children have to spend some of their holiday compulsorily lining the streets and marching in the procession past the saluting base on which the President stands with members of the foreign diplomatic corps and "prominent personalities". The people of Syria do not enjoy many free shows, and so they make the best of anything going to turn out and wave flags along the route of the procession.

Aleppo, large town of Syria.

The rest of the day is spent in official and unofficial visiting and family expeditions into the surrounding countryside. The parade starts at about seven in the morning, shortly after sunrise, as, even in April, it can be quite hot later in the day.

After Independence

With independence won, burning nationalism did not prove enough to give the new republic stability. The sense of national unity was not strong enough to make the people loyal to their government. This was partly because of the sense of local community encouraged by the French among the minorities in parts of Syria. Regime followed regime in a series of coups and counter-coups. The firework displays which in Damascus celebrate the advent of a new president became monthly if not weekly.

But, during the 1950s, the old-style nationalist politicians gradually lost to the more anti-West elements represented by the Baathists or Arab renaissance party. This party had one great advantage: it was not attached to any national leader or Arab state. Important Baathist movements developed in the 1950s in Lebanon, Jordan and Iraq as well as Syria. The party's disadvantage was that it was unable to win mass support, so that, when it did gain power, it held it only by extreme dictatorial methods. The

THE PALESTINE PROBLEM

Palestine or The Holy Land has a very real and special meaning to both Arabs and Jews — not to mention Christians. That is the root of the problem.

The Balfour Declaration (2 November 1917) sowed the seeds of a conflict which has not yet been resolved. It says:

His (Britannic) Majesty's Government view with favour the establishment in Palestine of a National Home for the Jewish People, and will use their best endeavours to facilitate the achievement of this object, it being clearly understood that nothing shall be done which may prejudice the civil and religious rights of existing non-Jewish communities in Palestine, or the rights and political status enjoyed by Jews in any other country.

In 1917 Palestine was not a country but part of the Ottoman Empire which all belonged to the Turks. They were fighting with the Germans against "The Allies", made up mainly of Britain and France, in what we know as the First World War, 1914-18. It was vital for The Allies that The United States of America come in on their side, and because Zionist Jews in America were so influential — politically and financially — they were able to make the Declaration a condition of American support.

The victorious Allies gave Palestine to Britain as a Mandate. Britain was bound to keep the promise of the Declaration to the Jews, but the fact was that

Israeli soldiers patrol East Jerusalem.

Arabs made up 98% of the population and owned 92% of the land. And so Britain tried to be "even-handed". Up until the Second World War in 1939 there were riots and rebellions by the Arabs against the British. The situation was given worldwide importance by the terrible revelations of the fate of the Jews in Hitler's gas chambers. It now seemed vital (even to some Arab sympathisers) that the Jews must have a home. Again, the American Zionists were able to exert pressure which resulted in the Partition Plan being passed in 1947 by a United Nations Resolution. The Arabs rejected this without question, but to the Jews half a loaf was better than no bread.

The British could cope no longer and pulled out. On the very next day the State of Israel was proclaimed by the Jews. Within three years the Jewish population had doubled, both because of the influx of Jews from abroad and because of Arabs being forced and encouraged to leave in large numbers. Arab refugees were housed in camps in neighbouring Arab countries. Resistance took the form of guerilla activity. The Palestine Liberation Organization was formed in 1964 and is the most moderate and effective of many Arab organizations.

Israel fought three major wars between 1956 and 1973, on the whole enlarging the territory which it had been assigned by Partition. But after the last one in 1973, Israel agreed to withdraw from some of its conquered lands. The Arabs had, this time, fought with new determination and used sophisticated weapons with much greater skill than before, and this shook public confidence in Israel for the first time. The Israeli Labour Party Government, in power since 1949, was blamed for not foreseeing the war and Mr Menahem Begin was able to form a new coalition government. The question of settlements caused division in the Knesset (parliament) and the main stumbling block was the 1977 Camp David Agreement with Egypt, because it tied in with the question of autonomy for Arabs on the West Bank (territory Israel won by fighting, not by partition). This question is still the subject of argument in the government: one side wanting to build the maximum number of settlements on the West Bank and the other side considering them illegal.

The primitive, almost mystical, belief that once the land is ploughed it becomes the permanent property of the farmer for endless generations to come is fiercely held by Jew and Arab. This also makes a solution which would satisfy both sides impossible.

Baathists tried twice unsuccessfully to unite Syria with Egypt (since Arab unity is the essence of their creed). The party split and a more radical group seized power in a coup which, for the first time in Syria's modern history, involved bloodshed. The new regime was dominated by men of the minorities, because it depended on the armed forces for support and much of the army recruiting was from the minorities. In general, conservative Muslims were against the new party which became more and more directly under the influence of the Soviet Union. The working classes were pro-Baath and the upper and middle class against. Naturally, the nationalization of the Arab-owned banks and various industries and the transfer of land from landlord to peasant was not popular with the landlords.

As time went on, the more Marxist and doctrinaire elements of the party were opposed by "nationalists" less interested in Marxism and more in improved relations with Syria's neighbours and an all-out fight against Israel. The leader of this group which still called itself the Baath party was Hafiz el Assad. After a prolonged struggle which included Russian threats to cut off arms supplies to Syria which Assad countered by getting them from China, he seized power. His first test as President was the war which was going on next door between the Palestinian guerillas and the Jordanian army. The Palestinians were trying to take over Jordan, to be able to fight the Israelis. Very realistically, Assad was against his tanks going in to support the guerillas because he did not think the Syrian army was ready to beat the Israelis.

In all the Middle East countries, the Palestinian question is the key to all politics. The signing of the Camp David Agreement between Egypt and Israel, which went some way towards a separate peace between the two countries, united the rest of the Arab countries against Egypt, in what they called a "steadfastness and confrontation front".

Though President Assad was returned in

Morning in central Aleppo.

These beehive houses are very typical of the country round Aleppo.

1978 for a further seven years, Syria is (once again!) showing signs of unrest and dissatisfaction. Orthodox Muslims (that is, not members of the Islamic minorities) are beginning to be tired of all the key posts going to Alawites — Assad's kinsmen. There have

SYRIA

Before 1918 the term "Syria" or "Greater Syria" was rather loosely applied to the whole of the territory which stretched from the Euphrates river to the Mediterranean and from the Sinai desert to the foothills of the Taurus mountains in Turkey. The present Syrian Arab Republic is much more limited, though an echo of the past remains in that a Syrian Arab is proud to come from the "heartland" — an honour which a Jordanian, a Palestinian or a Lebanese will certainly not deny him. Damascus, the capital of Syria, is claimed to be the oldest capital city in the world. Aleppo, two hundred miles to the north, may be even older.

Syria is about the size of Wales, about 71,000 square miles. About half of this is arable land and the rest consists of bare mountain, desert and pasture, suitable only for Bedouin. The population, including Palestinians (numbering nearly two million in 1977) was eight-and-a-half million in 1979. Of the total population in 1973 35.9% were aged under ten and 49% under fifteen.

Syria was at one time thought to have no oil, but in 1974, for the first time, this export won over its mainstay of cotton. Today, America and Canada have got concessions on a fifty/fifty profit-sharing basis with Syria, and Syrian oil has been found of a better quality than was once hoped for. Also Syria gets full payment of transit dues from three pipelines crossing her territory with crude oil from Iraq to be loaded on ships in Syrian ports.

Syria's main imports are machinery and electrical and manufactured goods and a few hours shopping in Aleppo or Homs will leave no doubt that nearly all the enamel teapots, plates, thermoses and countless toys and other plastic goods come from China.

been more and more assassinations of Alawites — the worst was in Aleppo a few years ago when sixty young cadets were massacred.

The Syrians expected things to change when independence came, and they were once more in control of their own destinies, but things were not as dramatic as expected. One great difference, however, was that domestic reforms in education and health and the position of women could now go ahead. In the past, when a Christian power was in control, it had always been afraid of offending the Islamic people by giving education to women, for example. Also, especially in the question of oil, foreign concessions had strangled the country's source of wealth and perhaps forced spending on military roads when schools and hospitals would have benefited the people more. After independence new ideas of limiting families were introduced which the mandate would never have dared institute. The death rate became much lower because of better health care and more modern hospitals and better countrywide hygiene.

Independence has not solved all problems at home. It is at once obvious to any casual visitor, who spends even a day in Damascus, that there are an awful lot of poor people about: six small boys rush up to carry your bag, or offer to show you the way, or clean your car. The streets are crowded with people standing about with nothing to do and this is not only because of the way of life in a hot country. The gap between rich and poor is getting wider because oil and good trade, in general, make the business-man richer and do not help the poor man. All too many poorly clad and hungry Middle Easterners see their wealthy compatriots enjoying big cars and big houses and every sign of prosperity, while very little of it seems to rub off on them. The middle class is very small.

Because fewer children and old people die,

the demand for food is getting more all the time — in spite of modern agriculture and new irrigation schemes. Russia has quite an influence and tries to encourage socialism, but up till now this has not had the effect of making life fairer for the masses.

Arabs find it hard to understand what the West means by "democracy" — i.e. "government by the whole people of a country, especially through representatives whom they elect". Elections have been imposed by foreign rulers for their own advantage, so that they can appear to be asking the will of the people. But illiteracy and difficulties of transport have made universal suffrage impractical and meaningless. Centuries of the nomadic and pastoral way of life have resulted in the deeply ingrained attitude that personality is all-important and it is the man rather than the system which really counts. Abstract ideas mean even less to the Damascus man in the street than the London one — unless personalised. Saladin, by his very personality and dynamic energy, managed to get near uniting the whole of the Arab world of his day where the mere theory of unity would not have been enough. In the same way, the Mongol Chief Genghis Khan, while he was in the prime of life, held an empire stretching from China to the Middle East. His name was on the lips of all the thousands he had conquered and who had probably seen him on his horse or heard from others who had. Nearer our day, Lawrence of Arabia gained a hold on King Feisal and his followers' imagination by his fair looks, his daring and his energy as well as his Arab dress.

Where there is no hereditary leader there has to be a strong army and it is the leaders of the army who become the strong men and the personalities. This means that a bright young man without money behind him can get on — and can even rise to be President of Syria, like Lieutenant-General Haffiz al Assad, who is a professional soldier. The army is the one area where money and/or family influence do not count. In this way it can happen that the more progressive ideas about man's equality evolve in the army. This happened in Egypt under President Nasser, and in Iraq. In Jordan the King wears military uniform very often and tries to look as military as possible.

The Dome of the Rock.

The Modern Arabs

Today, some Arabs are asking themselves why it is that, since the last century, there has been a decline in the "quality of life" and in the way they think of themselves and the rest of the world thinks of them. Why is it that, since the ninth century, the Arabs have not really been a great nation? Why do people who go to Spain and see Grenada and the Alhambra, or to Jerusalem to see the Dome of the Rock and other magnificent evidence of a glorious and dynamic past, have such difficulty in believing that it is really Arab work?

The Arabs, like the Turks and the Persians, are always acutely aware of their own glorious past and their main aim, since they became independent and more powerful because of the oil, is somehow to recover status and dignity and respect in the eyes of the West. During the Crusades, the struggle between the world of Islam and the West was a fight between equals. Both sides may well have hated each other, but there was always mutual *respect*. This is what the Arabs feel that they lost in the subsequent centuries. The European Christian powers became technically and materially more powerful. To the Empire-builders of the eighteenth and nineteenth centuries, the Arabs "lacked guts"; they had no "team spirit", and this attitude persists to a certain extent. Of course, the Arabs now do have the means to catch up technically and materially, but bad attitudes of mind take a long time to change.

The Arabs argue this way among themselves : Arab traditions are no good and it is better to follow Western ways — not necessarily communism but that is a possibility. Others say that the only way is to go back to being more strictly Muslim or Islamic. Go back to the strict veiling of women, praying more, being meticulous about pilgrimage and following to the letter all the teachings of the Khoran. There are also the moderates who wish to combine the two and have the best of both worlds.

What does not help is the modern Western view of themselves which Arabs get from the daily press and their dealings with Europeans. "We are only news as nomads, fanatics or shoplifters," one of them told a London journalist. The cover of the magazine, *Time Out*, in which this was reported, showed a typical Kensington, London, scene: the whole of a pavement outside a square garden is taken up with Arabs in various attitudes of prayer on prayer mats or headcloths spread on the paving stones, with their shoes placed neatly between the gutter and the double yellow line. The kneelers are in all sorts of dress from long gowns and baggy trousers to town suits. Parked alongside is the biggest and shiniest Rolls with the most British-looking chauffeur, one hand on the polished car. On his chubby, good-tempered British face is a smile of long-suffering bewilderment. The same confusion exists in the Middle East, only in reverse.

The monument to the Baathist Party in Baghdad, Iraq.

One of the great differences between the young Arab of today and his European friend is that the patriarchal family system is still very strong in Middle East society. The family expects the loyalty and support of all its members and, in return, provides security and protection. Family loyalty is stronger still than loyalty to nation, political party or religion. But, like the European youth of the 60s, young Arabs in the '70s and '80s are feeling the need to rebel and to break away from authority at home and outside the home. "The Angry Young Arab" is recognized everywhere. Gradually, the well-known extended family of grandparents and cousins is giving way to the nuclear family of parents and children. In the large towns such as Damascus and Aleppo, families are much smaller, and two or at most three children are the rule.

The young Arab today is more and more inclined to what some have called a specially Arab kind of socialism — neither Soviet nor Maoist communism, and certainly not socialism as the West understands it, but resulting out of the special social traditions of Islam. The growth of the Baath (Regeneration) Party in Syria and Iraq is one aspect of this. However, the history of Syria since the Baath Party came into power has shown that communism and socialism fit uneasily onto the Arab mentality. In the first place, an Arab is Muslim first and foremost, so how can he be a true irreligious communist? Two other snags we have already mentioned: the importance placed on the individual and the strength of the family. On the other hand, the Islamic religion lays great stress on everyone being equal before God. Arabs are reminded of this when they make the pilgrimage to Mecca and find themselves among thousands of Muslims all dressed the same and all with the same words from the Khoran on their lips.

But modern air travel and mutual business and cultural interests force East and West to meet in a way which has not been so intensive since the Arabs conquered Spain and went into France in the eighth and tenth centuries. Television is in even the poorest home — provided it has electricity — showing serials like the English *Forsyte Saga*. Because of the dramatic change in world status of the Middle East, because of oil money, there is now less need to dwell on the Golden Age of 900 A.D.

May

The Bedouin

"The merry month of May" sees the end of junketing in the Middle East. By the middle of the month every trace of green has disappeared, except from well-watered gardens.

Only the tougher flowers remain, like the boring asphodel and the wild white hollyhock, luminous in the sun in any uncut field.

The Bedouin and their flocks and herds wander over the fields of golden stubble, drawing closer in towards the towns as their stocks of water dry up; though some seek

Bedouin tents pitched in Wadi Rum, Jordan.

Travelling camels, Kings Highway, Jordan.

the cooler uplands. This is when townspeople are most aware of the Bedouin. But they rarely pass a balanced judgement on them. Their attitude is either one of exaggerated scorn or one of equally unreasonable romanticism. Both attitudes have some grounding in reality. Bedouins are quarrelsome, suspicious and limited in interest, and they totally lack "team spirit"; but they are also hospitable, brave and independent. Their faults and virtues complement each other and are a result of their background and history.

In Jordan, where so much of the land is dry, unwatered desert, and in north Syria, the Bedouins' black tents are stretched like grounded planes in sheltered folds of the countryside. These tents are made entirely of goat hair; from ancient times and until very recently they were woven by the women out of the only raw material at hand. On hand looms, set up in the open, long thin strips of cloth are woven, then stitched together and propped up on poles. There is no ridge-pole anchored by guy ropes. The cloth expands when wet and becomes waterproof in rain. "Beit al Shahir", as the tents are called, means in Arabic "house of hair" and they are ideal for the wandering life because they can so easily be rolled up. There is a special word in Arabic for the mark left by the tent on the ground after the camp has been struck — MADHRAB. In these days it is not so unusual to see the tent and the camel loaded together onto large lorries, to be taken from one camping site to another. Camels are still useful where there are no good roads.

Groups of tents vary in size from one or two to a great number when a tribe has gathered for a special purpose. Five or six tents form an average community. Several tents of the same tribe often join together when their inhabitants are closely related, on a seasonal basis, to exploit pasture or water. Larger groups only form in response to particular political or economic conditions. The space between tents is important because of the sanitation problem. L-sans are unnecessary in the sun and wind, but there must be space for the sweet desert air to do its work.

The tents make cosier homes than one would imagine and a fire can be lit inside. The tent is divided into two sections — the men's and the women's — by a wall of reed held together by gay patterns of wool. The best side is always towards the men. The whole family sleeps on the women's side. A man normally moves into a tent of his own when he gets married and sometimes an elderly female relative joins the couple. A sheikh or head of the tribe has a larger tent.

It is on the men's side that visitors are received, and that is where the coffee hearth is. The women are supposed to keep strictly to their side when their husbands are entertaining, but in practice they often find it necessary to peer over and to join in the conversation with shouted comments. As they are often able to overhear conversation in tents they visit, women are more well-informed than one might think. Like all Islamic women, they must always keep their heads covered in front of men, but in the energetic life they lead, it would be impossible for the face to be constantly veiled.

Bedouin woman.
▽

Coffee-Making and Hospitality

It is the host's job to make the coffee. The green unroasted coffee beans are probably kept in a decorated bag hanging from the tent pole. They are roasted fresh each time, in a thick iron pan with a long handle, over a fire made of dried camel dung or sweet-smelling wormwood. The roasted beans are pounded in a brass or stone mortar with a rhythmic beat which can be heard all over the camp, so that everyone knows visitors are present. Before the final brew is ready the coffee is poured from the big pot into a line of smaller pots. Cardamom is added.

Bedouin serving coffee, south Jordan.

The coffee is served with the left hand into the top one of a stack of small handle-less cups held in the right. A loud blurping sip is a polite sigh of satisfaction. Only a little is poured in each cup; it can be refilled three times, after which it is polite to refuse, with a little fluttering shake of the cup as one hands it back. (In towns and villages there is a watered-down version of the Bedouin coffee-drinking ritual. It is still the centre of all social gatherings.)

Hospitality in the desert is a recognition of want; it has grown into a social grace. In the old days, at least, a stranger or group of strangers came to the tent door because there was nowhere else to go. To turn a man away would have been equivalent to murder. Such a society, for its own sake, could not afford to be anything but hospitable. It is a routine imposed by the desert and, as such, it has existed from earliest times. Civilization elaborated on the code of the desert (it is still considered bad manners to let anyone leave the house without offering them a coffee, at least). Mohammed with his characteristically practical sense enforced the routine: "Whosoever believes in God and the day of resurrection must respect his guest"; mutual friendship comes from having eaten bread and salt together and a man who means to do harm will not sit down with his enemy. Killing a sheep or a goat is usually

kept for special occasions such as a wedding or a religious feast, but bread and eggs and yoghourt are almost always offered by the poorest tents — and the more swimming in grease the better.

The Origin of the Bedouin

The origin of the Bedouin is no more clear than the origin of the other tribes which have been milling round the area for so many thousands of years. It is best to imagine a continuous circular movement from the towns into the desert and back: in the market towns of Aleppo and Damascus, where life was easier, the population increased until there was unbearable overcrowding; the weaker people were forced further and further into the desert, and eked out their precarious farming by keeping livestock and breeding sheep and camels. So they came to depend more and more on their herds for a living. Sooner or later a convulsion from the overstraining town population flung them right out into the untrodden wilderness as nomads. But the desert also gets overpopulated from time to time: weaker tribes then find themselves elbowed to the edge of civilization and cultivation. They begin to grow corn, so they are now no longer Bedouin, but suffer, like the villagers, from the ravages of the Bedouin behind.

Camels

The economic life of the desert is based on the supply of camels. The camel is everything to the Bedouin: his means of conveyance, his food — milk and meat (occasionally), and he breeds and sells them. Though, these days, cars and lorries are often used where there are roads, there are still vast tracts of land where only the camel (and horse and donkey) can go. All the animals are sometimes loaded onto lorries and carried from one desert to the other. The camel carries a trough on his back, so that he can be watered at wells, as well as the family goods and women and children who cannot walk.

According to the latest statistics (for 1978), Iraq, Jordan and Syria still have enough camels to count in the "livestock" column. Iraq has by far the most and Lebanon and Israel none. There are 1000 words for camel in Arabic, and a Bedouin can tell by the tracks in the desert what sort of camel has walked there — a female camel, pregnant and tired, or a male camel in full vigour at the beginning of a journey, carrying no load . . . .

The Bedouin even today do not respect frontiers. During their seasonal migrations thousands of camels can be seen crossing from Syria to Iraq or into Jordan during the spring and autumn, driven by the Bedouin tribes which own them and depend on them for their livelihood. The camels are best bred on the rigorous upland pastures with their strong nourishing thorns.

Town Life

The circular movement from the desert into the towns and back again, which explains the existence of the Bedouin and which, in the past, might have taken a generation or two, has sometimes been disrupted and speeded up by the Arab-Israel war. For example, a family with many sons making a precarious living is suddenly driven off the land by war into a refugee camp on the outskirts of a large town like Amman. The sons, starting from scratch, get what jobs they can, which makes them rich or not. In the course of time the son working in a bank asks his boss to lunch — not only his boss but as many friends as his boss likes to bring, say two or three car-loads. The big cars edge into the narrow streets outside the brand new house which the refugee family have moved into since all the sons are bringing in good money. The garden is still raw, but a revolving water spray is helping the newly planted flowers in their struggle against the wind and sun and dust. Inside, the women of the party are taken into a room with mat-

Middle-class residential area, Amman, Jordan.

tresses round the walls, which are brilliantly painted green and decorated at the corners with a jolly flower design straight off a carpet. The women take off their shoes and squat more or less comfortably, disposing of their knees and legs as elegantly as possible. The men are in the next room, sitting on chairs, drinking whisky. After a time the banker brings whisky in to the women of his party, some of whom are having a hard time not knowing any Arabic. For the meal, all sit together on the floor on mattresses. A jug of water and basin and a towel are brought round for everyone to wash their hands. Then two young men of the family carry in a huge round copper dish on which are piled layers of flat bread and roast chickens, all soaked in a rich sauce of olive oil, onions and saffron. Urged on by the host and the sons, the guests — using their hands — pile their plates and set to. The family do not sit down with the guests but stand behind them. A few polite remarks are exchanged but conversation is not necessary. When the food mountain has diminished a little and everyone is sitting back replete, the dish is removed to the kitchen for the family, and the jug, basin and towel are brought round again. It is only now that the hostess — and mother of all the sons — appears, to be congratulated. She looks incredibly young and, though pretending to be shy for the sake of form, is really at ease and quite able to talk to any of the town guests who know a little

At home.

Arabic. She wears slacks and a bright silk blouse and her head is covered with a scarf, but not her face. All the family wear indeterminate modern clothes such as jeans or suits.

That same day the banker might go to another party at one of his colleague's houses, which would be furnished in the very latest style, and where manners, food and conversation would be cosmopolitan and indistinguishable from in any other well-off family in the Middle East or anywhere in the Mediterranean.

The modern Ministry of Planning building and the old houses of Baghdad, by the Tigris.

In spite of the sophistication, certain customs do persist. For instance, a guest must always refuse food at first and wait to be asked three times. A wife was heard to complain that her husband never bothered to do this and left his friends hungry, which meant that she had to do the ritual pressing. After a meal such as the one described above, it would not be impolite to lick one's fingers, and a gentle belch of appreciation is good manners. Naturally, sitting up at table and using forks and knives make finger-licking unnecessary.

The thousands of middle-class families living in towns like Damascus and Aleppo, mostly in modern flats, have more or less the same mixture of East and West. As entertaining is such an important part of life — so many of the feasts consist of visiting family and friends — even the smallest flat has a room set aside as a guest room. Sometimes the children sleep in a passageway rather than the family not have a "salon", as it is called. The television is in every home and on all the time — sometimes with the sound turned down. Programmes mostly come from England or America and Shakespeare plays are popular.

Middle East towns are a mixture of old and new, with modern flats towering above old houses and beautiful new suburbs surrounding and merging into old parts of the town which have not changed for hundreds of years. Every town has its "souks" or shopping areas and in Aleppo these consist of many miles of covered tunnel-like streets with stalls on either side in which the goods are stacked with absolutely no idea of display. The owner of the shop sits on a wooden platform in front of the hole which is his shop and anyone buying anything sits down, has a cup of coffee, passing a pleasant twenty minutes before completing the deal. This is what the West calls "wasting time". Arabs do not consider conversation a waste of time. They hate the foreigners' hectic hurry which, quite rightly, they see as impolite. In Eastern society man, or the

Selling a bit of everything in the souq in Samarra, just north of Baghdad.

Traditional fruit-juice stand in Damascus, Syria.

person, is all-important. He has not yet been cowed by machines and high-rise buildings. Visitors to Arab countries are always impressed by the people's human dignity. God made man and therefore he is valuable. Arabs are reminded of this five times a day.

Though high-rise flats and new roads give towns a more modern look these days, and horse-drawn carriages and some costumes have disappeared, you can still see such things as the letter-writers under their black umbrella (sunshade!), with their earnest clients sitting on a stool in front of them, dictating a business letter or marriage arrangement. Street cries are not so deafening as they used to be — they tend to be lost in the noise of traffic — but sweet melon sellers and the sellers of drinks still shout their wares. Fortune tellers tracing their designs in the trays of sand have disappeared; their place has been taken by "the stars"

LEISURE

Watching the world go by is what some Middle Easterners do best in their leisure time. To enjoy it, one has to have a relaxed view of time. The men spend a great deal of their day in cafés drinking coffee, playing tric-trac (or backgammon) or talking to their friends (very often about money), smoking hookahs. Women are never seen in cafés, though old women smoke hookahs in the home. Like most housewives, they are constantly employed caring for their families and homes. Their main leisure pursuit is talking; that is why they are so intensely interested in anything unusual that comes their way. They tear a foreign visitor apart — to satisfy their fierce curiosity. But now that television is in every home, this will gradually change.

The modern young man or woman in a larger Middle Eastern town has the same amusements as anyone around the Mediterranean where the climate allows one to be out of doors so much of the year. The heat in the summer means that the early mornings and the late evenings are the times for leisure activities, such as tennis or swimming or walking – and riding.

There is an Arabic word "kayef" meaning enjoyment. "He is making kayef" covers any sort of activity which is not actually work. It can apply to sitting with his family enjoying the company of his wife and children, taking them out in the family car to the mountains to enjoy the air and the water – both to drink and to watch. The actual "view" is not often appreciated. Middle Easterners have not our fanatical romantic appreciation of scenery. ("Mensara" is the Arabic word for a view or outlook.) The person next to them, the food, and drink, the price of the house and the land are much more absorbing. "Kayef" is always improved by music, and Arabic songs from popular singers are a background to life everywhere. Radios don't have to be turned down – the louder the better.

Smoking hookahs over a game of dominoes.

which appear each day in the papers, as they do in the West.

One great change over the last fifty years in big towns like Damascus or Aleppo is that now each town is approached by a grand avenue of palm trees and olianders. This would not have been possible in the days before there was plenty of water.

Towns like Damascus and Aleppo are surprising — something new happens round every corner: in an open space near the Aleppo castle Bedouin women in long black dresses, their heads wound in black turbans, make their camels kneel to load on the shopping they have bought in the dark vaults of the nearby souk. Town ladies, in high heels, their faces almost hidden in flattering see-through veils, teeter past them with hardly a glance. Men in striped silk "dressing gowns", huge cummerbunds round their waists and ordinary suit jackets over their gowns, their heads in fringed squares folded diagonally and held on with a black crown or "agal" as it is called, saunter past, some of them with linked little fingers. Boys on donkeys, urging them on with their bare heels, cause as much nuisance as they can. Live chickens, sheep and goats for sale, with legs tied together, pant, dumbly awaiting their inevitable fate.

MUSIC AND DANCING

Folk music and dancing have a very long tradition and are still very much alive.

The various musical instruments are the same in all the Arab countries with a few slight modifications. The most popular are the reed pipe or shibbabah, the drum or derbakkeh, the tambour or tambourine and the oud or lute which is the best-known in the West, because it lends itself best to solo performance. This instrument is a work of art in itself with its lovely wooden half-melon shape and mother-of-pearl inlay.

The actual music consists of motifs called maqamat, which are always played with improvisations according to the skill of the performer. This is where it differs from Western music with its set scores.

In the same way, formal concerts are not the rule. Music and dancing happen in a relaxed social atmosphere with eating and drinking, the audience moving about, talking, sighing and clapping spontaneously.

Dancing very often goes with this music; most well-known is the dabkeh. Here the dancers form an open ring led by the "waver" or "lawwih" with a coloured handkerchief in his right hand, and the singer in the centre of the ring. As the steps of the dance quicken, with high spots in the song, the "waver" breaks away into short impromptu dances on his own. In some Arab countries women dance with the men; in others they perform on their own. The famous "belly dance" is quite different from the dabkeh, as it requires training and is done by a professional dancer.

Cars hoot all the time, their sleek modern streamline smothered in feathers, mirrors, and bead necklaces — a good helping of blue beads to bring good luck. Cars take people to the more modern part of the city which might seem undistinguishable from Europe — except that in the cafés only men sit all day, playing backgammon, and in the streets a lone woman is an oddity. Every-where there is a strong smell of roasting meat and baking bread, mixed with petrol, urine and rotting vegetables and rubbish. Everywhere is the noise of people talking at the tops of their voices, shouting over the constant car horns. A traveller arriving in a Syrian town needs sun glasses for the blind-ing white sunlight and ear plugs too — and safety belts for crossing the streets! Pave-ments are almost as hazardous as the road: nut sellers perch on the edge with their round trays resting on three-legged stands. If the police come along, the round trays are switched onto heads in a trice and all the outfit is moved to the next corner. Café chairs encroach onto the pavements until customers are nearly sitting in the gutter. The water which is constantly sprinkled between the tables, to keep the dust down, can give you a shower-bath. Added dangers here are the barbecues emitting sparks and ash as they are fanned energetically by the ubiquitous little boy. Little boys are the oil that makes the wheels go round in Syria and, in fact, throughout the Middle East — they are always on hand to take messages, bring an extra glass of water, dust off a chair, watch a car in case any one bumps it while the owner is away . . . . This is not to men-tion the professional little boys who have

West Jerusalem.

huge baskets strapped to their backs, to carry shopping home, or who man shoe-shine boxes — another hazard on the pavements.

All this is bearable and even enjoyable because towns in the Middle East are still small enough to be easily walked through, as in Medieval times in Britain. Replanning is a threat, with new roads driven through an organic mass of houses which have grown up gradually over hundreds of years. Along the new streets high-rise blocks of flats are built and this destroys many little neighbour-hoods, each with its own café, grocer, baker, bath-house, meeting place. Also, the con-crete high-rise flats are hot in summer because they are no longer built for shade, with inner rooms round courtyards, and deep-shaded windows. Not by any means do all houses have air-conditioning. Europeans, used to gas laid on, will be surprised to find that all households in the Middle East, even in the big towns, cook on camping gas. Great round holders being delivered are a well-known sight. Electricity is for lighting, but many households have no electricity. Winter heating is by oil central heating or oil stoves. Other public services which we usually take for granted are innovations in big towns like Aleppo and Damascus, but not usual in the smaller towns and villages. Cess pools and wells are still part of any building more than fifty years old. Rubbish collection is still often by a man with a donkey who empties messy tins of fly-ridden rubbish into the saddle-bags. (In the melon season the donkey eats the skins.) This does not happen any more in the most modern centres and suburbs of all the big towns.

Servants are becoming more and more hard to get in the big towns and are now not called servants but "helpers" or "workers". Their hours are regulated so that they can no longer be exploited. Also, as so many towns-people live in flats, the "helpers" do not now live in as they used to, almost becoming part of the family. In the last generation it was still possible to buy a "slave" or an unwanted girl from villagers or Bedouin.

June

The Death of the Prophet

The Prophet Mohammed died on 8 June in the year 632 A.D., but although his followers were stunned at the time, of course, and the question of who was to succeed him was vitally important, this is not a day remembered in the Muslim calendar, in the same way as Christians remember the crucifixion of Jesus. Muslims believe that on the night of Mohammed's death the tree of life is shaken. On its leaves it bears the names of all the people on earth. The names which fall to the ground can expect death before the year is out.

The dead lie and expect the Day of Judgement. The way the Khoran describes the Day of Judgement is, on the whole, not very different from what the Christians and the Jews believe. There will be a great noise and the sound of enormous trumpets. The stars will be darkened and the walls of the houses will swell and boil and the earth tremble. The damned will go to "gehenna" or "the fire". Special angels will be assigned to torture them. They will be loaded with chains and iron collars, and jets of fire and molten bronze will be turned on them. When their skin has been burned off, it will be replaced so that the pain will be never-ending. Sometimes it will be terribly cold, but the brackish water they will be given to drink will be boiling hot. They will be made to eat fruit from a very bitter tree and this will gnaw their entrails. They will beg in vain for mercy. But the blessed will be rewarded, like the Christian pious. There *is* a difference though: besides dwelling forever in gardens, by springs of water, forever eating the most luscious and juicy of fruits, there will be other delights, which are not so graphically described by Christian theologists. The women, for instance, are ever young, ever virgin, ever seductive, with modest looks but shapely breasts and huge languishing eyes — "hur al 'in", which is Arabic for "gazelle-like eyes of a beautiful black". From this comes the word *"Hoori"*, a young and beautiful woman. Muslim paradise is inhabited by *Hooris*.

Mohammed's night journey to heaven is also celebrated in June. The legend is that he made this journey, after his death, mounted on "Burac" — a winged horse with women's attributes — his body all the time lying peacefully on his bed. He journeyed through seven heavens and in each one he met different prophets who had gone before him and even the Angel Gabriel, who expounded to him the secrets of heaven and hell.

Mohammed's death and night journey are commemorated by women visiting graves and putting flowers there.

Aisha

Mohammed died in the arms of his second and most beloved wife, Aisha. Her death is also remembered this month. His first wife, Khadija, was more of a mother figure for the poor orphan Mohammed; he was very fond of her, too. She was a rich woman and employed him to look after her caravans, and perhaps he first went to Syria for her. Some accounts say that the penniless young man of twenty-five had to get Khadija's father drunk before he would consent to their marriage. But she was his first convert and he always said that he would live with her in paradise in a house of reeds. However, she gave him no children.

MOHAMMED

Mohammed was born in the small oasis town of Mecca in the region known as the Hijaz in about the year 571 A.D. There were some nice well-watered valleys here, where agricultural towns had been since ancient times, but the greater part of the country of his birth was arid desert crossed by caravan routes, the habitual paths taken by the camel trains carrying merchandise from India and China between the ports of Southern Arabia and those on the Mediterranean, from where it could be shipped to Europe. Most of the population were nomads or Bedouin who wandered the desert according to where their herds could find food, and made raids on more fertile lands.

Mohammed's father died soon after Mohammed was born and his mother when he was only a few years old. In those times it was considered good for all children — even the ones with parents — to be sent for short periods to live with the Bedouin, to be toughened up by the Spartan way of life and (most important) to hear the Arabic language spoken at its purest. So Mohammed naturally spent a lot of his time in the tents and he evidently liked it, because he eventually became the leader of trading caravans and so travelled a long way from home. On these journeys he must have had plenty of opportunity to talk with Christians and Jews and to get a good working knowledge of both religions.

"Islam" was the name of the new religion which now became as important as the two already mentioned. The Five Pillars of Islam spell out its basic principles in the Khoran, the sacred book held to be inspired by God. Like the Jews and the Christians, the Muslims, or followers of Islam, believed in one God.

Mohammed called himself the "Messenger of God". There had been many "messengers" or prophets — perhaps as many as 40,000; Christ was one, as well as Abraham. None of them (including Mohammed) was considered divine, as Christ was by the Christians. That would have been considered blasphemy.

Mohammed impressed his new religion on his followers by sheer force of personality; it was a feat in itself to get them to submit to the discipline of praying — and washing — five times a day. And it was this new discipline which gave the Muslims an impetus and an enthusiasm, the first wave of which lasted well over a hundred years.

Pilgrims to Mecca circling the Ka'aba, the cubic building which houses the black stone — held most sacred by Muslims because kissed by Mohammed. Before his time it contained many other stones, then worshipped as gods. Mohammed threw them all out.

Mohammed was about fifty when he married Aisha. Her own account relates

The Messenger of God married me when I was six years old. The wedding was celebrated when I was nine. My mother came to me while I was playing with my friends on a swing. Some women washed my head and made me beautiful. I was not frightened except in the morning when the Messenger of God came and they gave me to him.

The little girl was allowed to keep her dolls. The marriage was consummated when she was thirteen.

Aisha used to ride with her husband on his campaigns, in a covered litter or "howda", swaying on the back of a camel. All women in those days travelled like this; they must have been the object of much fantasy among the men. Especially Aisha. There is a touching account in her own words of how, one day, she had got down from her camel "to fulfil a need" and lost her shell necklace. While she was feeling about in the sand for it, the camp departed, thinking she was inside her litter. Left alone, she wrapped herself in her cloak and lay down on the ground. Soon, one of the men in the caravan, who for some reason had dropped behind the previous day, found her. Aisha explains: "now he had seen me before we were instructed to wear the veil" (when she was a child). He recognized her and cried out: "the wife of the prophet! Why have you been left behind?" "But I spoke no word to him." When they got back to the caravan, there was a scandal. As a modern writer comments, "It was and still is true to say of the Arabs . . . that love or sexual attraction is regarded as a force of nature of such power that no will is strong enough to fight it. When a man and a woman find themselves alone and without witnesses nothing can keep them from each other's arms . . . . Simply being together amounts to making love" in the eyes of scandal-mongers.

The Prophet had fifteen to twenty wives in all, as well as countless concubines, who produced a total of seventeen sons — the daughters are not counted. To prevent anyone seeking to gain power by marrying one of Mohammed's widows, all the wives were given the courtesy title of "mother of the Muslims" and so, as the Khoran said, "their widowhood became perpetual". No Arab could marry a woman he called "mother".

Mohammed's attitude towards women was one of great respect. Before Mohammed, infant girls were often killed at birth, but the Khoran said that they should be spared. This was partly to emphasize that God would provide for all, including women. On the whole, the Khoran tried to be fair to women and to treat them as individuals. It said that the dowry was to be the property of the woman and not of her father-in-law. Also, the pagan rule that a man must marry all his father's widows except his own mother was abandoned. The notorious verse saying that a man can marry up to four wives goes on to say "if you can be fair to them all". It may be that, in times of war and hardship, when there were many more women than men, it was an obligation for a man to take as many under his wing as possible. A survey in Egypt in 1976 showed that only four per cent of men had more than one wife.

Women in the Middle East

The Arabs are always being asked about the status of their women and how much and how soon they will be emancipated. The veiled woman is regarded with a mixture of pity and horror and not a little curiosity by Western society. Quite often it is forgotten that women in Western society were only emancipated fairly recently. It is not all that long since the first woman was admitted to our parliament. Women's liberation has advanced further in some Arab countries than others. It is often a question of education. Most Arab countries which have the money are keen on educating their women,

The town of Hama in central Syria is traditionally the most conservative. Women cover their heads with black veils.

Writing class for women in Damascus.

but sometimes they have not advanced socially and the university girls then have to come home to put on their veils again. This can happen in some conservative families in Damascus, Aleppo and Hama. But things are bound to alter in the next generation, because of the change in the family which, though still strong, is gradually losing its hold.

At the moment, especially in the countryside, there are many heads of families who believe that primary education is still quite enough for girls. In spite of the modern look of jeans and discos and some girls learning to be engineers and entering all sorts of

masculine professions, a girl of any age has to ask her parents before she can marry. Virginity is still considered extremely important. The general view is that the sooner a girl is married the better, to keep her out of mischief. Also, the younger she is, the better she can be moulded by her husband. Many Syrian men do the shopping so that their wives will not be tempted to stray. It really depends on the character and liberality of a man how a girl fares. But . . . "If a woman loves you she can open countless doors to you but if she hates you with a spider's web she can build an iron wall across your path." (Old Arab Proverb!)

Marriage

The Islamic faith is a strong framework supporting every aspect of life in the Middle East. Modern life is imposed on the framework, but does not change it. Marriages are not always arranged, but the family tie is strong: if two brothers, for instance, marry two sisters and one couple is unhappy, then the other couple, however happy, has to split up too. This was the plot of a recent television play in Jordan. Divorce is allowed,

42

but it is well-known that Mohammed considered it the one "allowed" rule he was least fond of. Divorce is not easy because, when a man marries, he takes on not only the girl but her whole tribe or family — and so he has them to reckon with if he considers leaving her. The marriage contract is in two parts : in the first, the father of the man gives the bride a sum of money to pay for her clothes, the wedding feast and all the expenses; the second is an agreement about how much the husband will pay if there is a divorce. These days the bride is often consulted about the sums she considers proper. Usually she asks for a lot of money in the first part, and hopes that the second will not be needed.

The wedding ceremony consists of beribboned motorcades winding through the town, making as much noise as possible. Men shoot blank shots into the air, women utter their shrill lé lé lé, which they do on every happy occasion. Feasting goes on for three days in the husband's house and, in modern times, the bride wears a white wedding dress and rings are exchanged, though this is not a Muslim custom. In Syria there is a special wedding soup called "fette", made of garlic and yoghourt and sheep's trotters.

Birth Customs

Though births in villages and in the desert still occur in the home, assisted by old women, in towns they usually take place in hospitals. The mother and all the guests who visit her drink "karawiya", made of ground rice seasoned with caraway seed. This drink is supposed to benefit the milk supply. Chicken soup is considered strengthening for the mother in these times and she is kept on a constant diet of this.

Except sometimes in villages, boy babies are circumcised very soon after they are born, by the doctor in the maternity hospital. In villages it is performed by the traditional barber, when the boy is about five. He is dressed grandly and rides on a white donkey, followed by a dancing, singing crowd of men playing drums and pipes.

Though it is said to be no longer a disgrace to have girls, sons are still more prized for the simple reason that in Middle East society (as elsewhere) they have more earning power. A visitor found her friend, who had given birth to a girl, lying on a mattress on the floor instead of on a bed, as she would have done if the baby had been a boy. In towns, families are often limited to four, as the flats are small, but in the villages a man applying for a job will boast that he has thirteen mouths to feed — namely nine children (including the girls), his or his wife's

A swaddled baby in his cot, in a northern Syrian village.

parents, besides himself and his wife. Sometimes the smallest town flats can contain an extraordinary number of people, who spread their beds upon the floor in every room when night comes. Middle East bedding consists of a kind of cotton duvet or "yorgan", which is a heavy solid cotton eiderdown with the sheet stitched on. This is folded up and put away in a wall cupboard together with the very hard cotton-filled pillows.

Death Customs

There are no undertakers in the Middle East — yet. When a person dies, the relatives ask the mosque to find them someone to wash the body (according to sex) and to come and read some verses from the Khoran. The body is then taken on a stretcher (there are usually no coffins) to the mosque and then to the grave. The funeral must be within three days. After the funeral, relatives and friends meet in one house, or the men in one house and the women in another. On feast days the graves are visited. Sometimes families pay professionals to read verses of the Khoran. There is a sad story of a poor widow who could afford only about two and a half pence. She listened to the verse she had paid for being read, then objected that it was one of the gloomier ones, describing hell fire. "What do you expect for that money?" answered the man. "Descriptions of heaven?"

The laws of inheritance dictate that a man must leave a third of his wealth to some institution outside his family. The rest must be divided among his children, his wife and his mother. So there can be no landed gentry in the Middle East. This makes buying and selling land very complicated and law suits go on for generations.

July

The heat was as loud as some glorious noise or din. It echoed or reverberated off the paving stones of the court which was so hot that one could hardly keep one's feet on them ...

Sacheverell Sitwell, who wrote this in 1957, had clearly chosen the wrong time of year to visit the Middle East. But Muslims have no choice. Summer heat makes life difficult for all but the rich and idle who can sleep all day.

Ramadan

At present, the month of fasting, Ramadan, falls in one of the hottest months of the year.

Ramadan is the most sacred month in the Muslim calendar and the only one mentioned by name in the Khoran. During the whole lunar month, every day from sunrise till sunset, the faithful must abstain from food and drink and all sensual pleasure. The most scrupulously devout will not even smell a flower. The idea is to make an offering of fidelity to God, to do something to show devotion. It is not quite the same as the Christian Lent, because the idea is not self-denial but giving to God. Mohammed copied the idea of the fast from the Jews, who kept the fast of Yom Kippur, but he made it a month long, to distinguish his religion from theirs.

Islam

Mohammed called his faith "Islam", which means "submission". "Muslim" is another form of the same root and means "one who submits". The five basic principles of Islam are: (1) there is no God but God and Mohammed is the prophet of God; (2) both men and women pray five times a day — at sunrise, mid-day, afternoon, sunset and evening. The times of prayer are usually given from a minaret in the local mosque. The ritual is called "salat". The private and personal form of praying which can take place spontaneously at any time of day is called "du'a". The worshipper must be in a state of purity, in a ritually clean place, and facing the direction of Mecca, the birthplace of the Prophet. In the desert, where there is no water, it is enough to simulate washing with sand. Prayer mats are necessary because Muslims consider it a desecration to step on holy ground in shoes. In the Bible, God tells Abraham to take the shoes off his feet because the ground is holy. A man can pray on his mat and then roll it up and put it aside till the next time, out of the way of trampling feet. (3) The third principle is to fast during the month of Ramadan; (4) the fourth to give alms; and (5) the fifth to make the pilgrimage to Mecca if and when possible.

These five basic principles of Islam are in the Khoran, which is believed by Muslims to be directly inspired by God, and to be the very words of God, so that the book itself is considered sacred. There is also the Hadith (sayings), which are reports of the actions and sayings of the Prophet. These were handed down by oral tradition and put in writing after Mohammed's death, and are not quite so holy as the Khoran, because not the actual words of God.

The word Khoran means "recitation". "Recite in the name of thy God who created thee and I recited." These are the first words of the Khoran. Traditionally, it was on a

Exhausted by the fast of Ramadan and the summer heat, a woman sleeps on the pavement in Kerbela, Iraq.

night during Ramadan that the Angel Gabriel first appeared to Mohammed, shook him roughly by the throat, and commanded him to recite. After a time, Mohammed got used to these "happenings", though, each time, his face was covered in sweat and he was seized with violent shuddering, then lay unconscious for an hour as if in a drunken stupor. He heard strange noises like the sound of chains or bells or rushing wings. "Never once did I receive a revelation," he is reported to have said, "without thinking that my soul had been torn away from me." He learnt to listen more before uttering. Sometimes he stammered in his eagerness and was reproved by the Angel: "Do not wag your tongue." Some people think that the odd detached letters which appear at the beginnings of some of the verses represent this stammering.

The Prophet may have had hallucinations which contained memories of things described to him by Christians and Jews during his long caravan journeys under the moon and the stars. Some people who claim to know nothing about music are capable of writing down Beethoven-like symphonies as if these had been dictated to them. Great mystics like Mohammed must experience this in a nobler form because of the special kind of person they are. Because they see things more clearly than most people and

Midday prayers at the shrine to the Prophet Hussain, Kerbela, Iraq.

sometimes express what they see in rather exaggerated words and gestures, they can appear mad.

Mohammed's utterings when he was in one of his "states" were taken down during his lifetime on a variety of materials: skin, papyrus, the blade bones of camels — whatever came to hand. Later, all the suras or verses, except the first one, were arranged with the longest ones first and the shortest at the end. The language is very old and the meaning often obscure; but the Khoran is still a unique book and it keeps the Arabs' pride in their traditions alive and their language pure.

During the World Festival of Islam, held in London a few years ago, a beautiful poster was produced on which was printed the whole of the Khoran in small but legible letters. This made it easy to see the shortest verses at the beginning and the longest ones at the end. This poster contains nothing but what the Muslims believe to be the actual words of God, transmitted through his Prophet Mohammed. A poster with the whole of the New or Old Testaments of the Bible would not be possible, because of their length, and it would contain a lot of "dross" in the form of repeats of the same story. The actual words of Christ sometimes differ in the four Gospels, which are four different accounts of his life written after his crucifixion.

The Mosque

As well as being the "place of prostration", the mosque is also the centre of society, like a Roman forum or a Greek agora. The pulpit used to be a platform from which important announcements were made, not always to do with religion — news of the appearance of new governors or new statements of policy. The man in the pulpit held a sword or a bow as a badge of office. The mosque is always open and there is nothing against transacting business there. In early times it was a court of justice and often had schools connected with it. The interior of a mosque is simple and austere, with rich carpets sometimes providing the only decoration. People sit on the floor or kneel. There is no altar or sanctuary. The Imam is the man officially

Inside the Ummayad Mosque in Damascus, founded in the seventh century. The open courtyard occupies an area of 15,700 square metres.

appointed to take the prayers, but any Muslim who knows the ritual may take over.

The Id el Fitr

A three-day feast called the Id el Fitr or Breakfast Feast follows the month-long fast of Ramadan. The beginning and ending of the holy month depends on the sighting of the new moon, and this is not always easy because of weather conditions. Of course, everyone is eager to see the crescent at the end of the month and to begin the days of feasting, and sometimes there can be false alarms. It can happen that the feast begins a day later in Damascus than Cairo. In modern times the radio broadcasts the good news; fifty years ago it was the cannon's boom.

Evening prayers in the mosque. ▷

The Id el Fitr is celebrated with an especially grand breakfast. Guests note the number of different dishes on the table and compare them to their own table, and other places they visit. There are always coloured eggs and the lighter kinds of sweets, like milk puddings stuck with green pistachio nuts or sprinkled with cinnamon. Otherwise the feast is marked in the usual ways: new clothes for everyone, visiting and fairs. If the feast comes in the summer months, daytime activities are less, because of the heat.

August

Summer Heat

The heat has now settled in earnest on the land. The Armenians in the Middle East have a festival which dates from pagan times called "Vartevar", which is celebrated with a whole day of water fighting. As you can imagine, this is a great time for children; to get wringing wet is not really a hardship when the temperature is in the upper 90s. Those who can afford it have long since left for the mountains — any elevated place where there might be a chance of a breath of fresh air. It is a time of hot winds off the desert called the "hamseen", which can blow for three days and nights and are made the excuse for every kind of bad temper and neurotic behaviour.

Slowing up is the way all hot-country dwellers cope with heat. The Middle East has a great variety of climates — from snow at the top of Mount Sannin from December to May, to 140° in Iraq in the summer — but in general, it is warmer than in most of Europe. Schools have closed by the beginning of June, and during the summer, offices and shops have a long rest in the middle of the day. Perhaps a European will pride himself on staying at his desk throughout a broiling afternoon, but he is not admired for this by his Middle Eastern colleagues. As archaeologists trying to run a dig in the summer months have found, it is almost impossible to keep an Arab digger or basket boy upright in the heat of the day — his instinct is to stretch out! When the sun is at its height, every scrap of shade is occupied by one or more reclining figures with only the hard ground and perhaps a stone for a pillow. Dogs and cats, donkeys and horses slumber too. Only the flies and the mosquitoes remain active — people seem to be able to wave them off automatically without actually waking up.

Air-conditioning is still not universal, by any means, but the hot air can be kept out of the house by shutting all the windows and shutters early, while it is still cool. Water is sprinkled on the ground inside and outside the house and, of course, there are cold drinks with tinkling ice. Fruit drinks such as "sherbets" originated in hot countries. A very refreshing drink is "iran", like a very liquid yoghourt. This used to be sold in the streets before 7Up and Coke took over. In the days before fridges snow used to be stored in pits in the mountains covered with dead leaves and branches of pine. In the summer great blocks would be sawn out and

A dripping ice-cart in Kerbela, Iraq. The temperature was 49°C.

carried down to the hot cities on donkey back — sometimes a day's journey away. A lot of it melted, but enough was left to bob about in cool drinks. In the desert, Arabs do not "cast clouts" when May is out, but put more on, to protect themselves from the heat. But Arab sheikhs will sometimes come to town in special, very thin, almost see-through "abayahs" or fine black-wool cloaks embroidered in gold, which look magnificent floating out behind over their long "night-gowns" and flowing head-dresses of black-and-white or black-and-red.

Gardens

In extreme hot weather those who have to remain in the towns really appreciate their gardens. The main difference between the Western and the Middle Eastern attitude to gardens is that in the Middle East no flower without a perfume is considered any good. Also there is not the Western fixation on lawns. The water shortage makes them very expensive and difficult to grow. Even in front of luxury flats in Damascus the grass is not at all like the grass we know — coarse and dark green. Modern town gardens consist of low stone walls and paved areas with perhaps a fountain and plants in pots and tins set about the place. The rose and jasmine, carnation and honeysuckle are the favourite flowers. At night the whole of Damascus is jasmine-scented, even with the car fumes. There is a beloved flower, often grown in tins, called the "fillé". This looks like a small pale yellow rose but has shiny bright green leaves and no thorns. Of course, it has a heavenly smell, heavy and sweet. It is so precious that sometimes the leaves are decorated with gold-leaf. It is not unusual to see a man holding a rose or a "fillé" in his hand, sniffing at it, or even with it stuck into his head-dress. Many kilos of a very highly perfumed pink rose, common as hedges in the market gardens, are turned into jam — in the Hotel Baron in Aleppo and in private houses — as we make marmalade every winter.

In villages there is not very much in the way of gardens. The housewife is supposed to have other important things to do, but sometimes, there are giant orange marigolds and zinias to add a crude splash of colour and bright dahlias alongside the vine-covered trellises to the mud huts, and the morning glory climbs everywhere. Some trellises support a peculiar gourd, shaped like a wine decanter, with a bulbous bottom and a long thin neck. These gourds are put to all sorts of uses: as musical instruments, rattles — or they make huge ladles for pouring water from one can to the other at bath-time. Another trellis may hold a loofah plant (the loofahs looking like huge cucumbers when fresh), so two plants supply basic bath requirements. In towns the public baths are still much used by the poorer people, but in the villages a great round, thick copper basin, about 20 centimetres deep and 75 centimetres across is what everyone uses as a bath. This is kept in a paved room, next to the lavatory — which is a hole in the ground flushed by a rubber hose from a nearby tap. More luxurious bathrooms have a wood-burning or oil-burning stove to heat the water in a cauldron on the top. A gourd like the one described is used to pour water from the tin into the "tesht", and the "loofah" scrubs the dirt off. Other "bath aids" are a low wooden stool for sitting on in the middle of the "tesht", and "kabkhabs", or clogs, to keep clean feet off the wet floor. A generation ago (and perhaps even now) houses could have a European bathroom with a bidet and all the latest furnishings, as well as a "maid's bathroom".

Water and Rivers

The sound of buckets plunging down a well; the clank of metal against metal as the one coming up bumps against the one going down; water dripping into the dark depths — all magnified by echo — these are the sounds of summer. On a hot day, just to hear water being poured from the well bucket into a pail makes one feel cool.

The Arabs appreciate water as French-men do wine. They speak of its lightness, which is a sign of wholesomeness and

digestibility. Aleppo poets talk of the excellent quality of its water, preferring it to the waters not only of the Abarna and the Pharphar (rivers of Damascus) but also of the Nile. Aleppo has no big rivers; the Kuwaik is almost a joke, except in the flood season. Since ancient times the town has relied on a very efficient system of pipes which has brought water from a spring about 18 kilometres away. Many of the houses (except the modern ones) have vast underground cisterns called "sahreegg" which preserve the rainwater. This means that roofs are carefully swept at the beginning of winter and kept out of bounds to children until the summer. In Aleppo, the man with an assorted collection of iron hooks and chains for getting lost objects out of wells was until very recently a familiar sight.

The Euphrates, the Tigris, the Abarna and the Pharphar all run from north to south. The Orontese runs from south to north, and for this reason is called the "Asi" — which means "mad" in Arabic. The Euphrates and the Tigris are called "the twin rivers", but they have distinct individualities. For instance, the Euphrates has no tributaries. The Tigris, swifter than its twin, does not form swamps or change its course. It carries more water and the current is much faster. Upstream navigation is impossible on both rivers.

Spring always used to be an anxious time as, following the melting of the snow in Turkey, both rivers rose — the Tigris in April and the Euphrates in May. The Tigris was known to rise at the rate of 30 cm an hour. Floods of ten metres were known. The rivers could also suddenly change their course, so that a flourishing city might suddenly be left high and dry. This happened to Nippur, the capital of Sumer, a garden city on the Euphrates over three thousand years ago. The Sumerians were a civil-servant-type of people who left thousands of clay tablet records. The violent yearly behaviour of the two rivers demanded a careful irrigation

△
Date palms line the Euphrates in southern Iraq.

The Euphrates dam.   ▷

system, and thousands of well-organized people to run it. A super-civilization grew up. The pre-history of the Middle East is based on this civilization between the "twin rivers".

Nowadays, since the oil money really began to flow, there has been much more money available for ambitious dams and flood control systems. This has ended serious flooding.

A great dam has been built on the Euphrates which has solved the problem for Syria's farming of the wide differences in rainfall each year. The dam provides nearly all the country's electricity, as well as irrigating large areas of desert. Constructing the dam involved building a lake 80 kilometres long — called after President Assad of Syria; flooding a hundred riverside villages;

Women peasants till new land irrigated by the   ▷
Euphrates dam.

and building a completely new town to house the ten thousand workers who built the dam in ten years. The dam itself is nearly 5 kilometres across, and anyone standing on top of it can feel the vibration of the mighty turbines churning away and see the rippling lake stretching away to one side and the mighty river foaming through eight sluices on the other. There are eight turbines in the mighty marble hall below the dam, "consecrated to the gods of electricity and power". On each turbine top are inscribed the words Leningrad or Novosibirsk. One cannot help thinking of the bricks inscribed "Nebuchadnezzor made this palace" which have recently been fished out of the Tigris.

The mad and eccentric Orontes flows past the towns of Homs and Hama. Hama is full of the sound of its great wooden water-wheels — the grumblings of such wheels were well-known in Roman times, when they were

The giant water-wheel in Hama.

an important part of irrigation. The great wooden wheel at Hama, which raises water into an aqueduct which spreads the water to the crops, may have been part of the work of Saladin, who restored the town in 1178, after it had been destroyed by an earthquake. As big as a fairground wheel, it is turned effortlessly by the river. As you watch the dripping wheel, you are gripped by a sense of futility — so much of the water seems to fall wastefully back into the stream and can it really be worth all these countless years of turning and groaning? Little boys jump into the river for a breath-taking game: they catch hold of one of the projections of the wheel as it comes up and ride up with it right over the top where they jump 15 metres into the swirling froth below.

Christ and John the Baptist immersed the faithful in the waters of the river Jordan, thereby making the small insignificant stream world-famous. No one who has not seen the Jordan can possibly imagine how poorly it compares with its image.

September

If the first rains have not come before the end of September, people begin to talk darkly of earthquakes and unnatural happenings. But usually, in about the third week, the skies begin to cloud over, the first sprinkling of rain falls, and the first cool breeze brings out the first woolly and the first blanket on the beds. The damp earth smells delicious and the thirsty fields suddenly produce large yellow autumn crocuses. But the thrill of putting on raincoats and paddling through delicious puddles of cool mud is

tempered by school. The long summer holiday is over and school-time has undeniably come again.

Education in the Middle East

Education all over the Middle East is free and compulsory from the age of seven. The stages are primary, preparatory and secondary — and then university. Not surprisingly, in a land where more than half the population is of school age, one is always conscious of crowds of children in uniform, wending their way back and forth from school, with large heavy satchels on their backs. Even the youngest seem to have a great deal of homework. Conscientious mothers spend hours at home helping their children. Television is a menace, and it has not yet been developed as an educational aid.

Classes are large compared to ours: 50/60 pupils. As there are not enough schools, classes are on the shift system. The first shift works from 7 a.m. to about 11.30 and the second from 1.30 p.m. to 4 p.m. Therefore, school dinners are unknown. Boys and girls are together in the lower classes of the schools but, higher up, they work and play separately. The boys play football and do physical training and the girls play basketball. There is swimming, which is also segregated.

Textbooks are plentiful and some of them are printed locally. There are a lot of scholarships offered by foreign powers such as Russia, France and Britain. As to punishments, beating is illegal (in Jordan) and all agree that bullying is not such a problem as it is in the West. Foreign teachers are often surprised at the politeness of the pupils. This is probably also due to family discipline. Exams are not always fair and there have been instances of the son of the Minister of Education or some other official being given a special prize when he was certainly not the top of the class.

Every Middle East child, whatever his nationality or religion, must take Arabic as his first language. The Arabic alphabet reads from right to left, without capitals. The consonants and vowels at the end of words are written in full. Dots and small loops above or below the line indicate mid-word vowels and they can be omitted. For instance, "tray" would be written "tray", but "terrible" would be written in Arabic "trbl". Most of the letters have three forms, according to whether they occur at the beginning, the middle or the end of a word. Scripts are square ("kufic") or rounded

Back to school, Jordan.

BOOKS AND PAPERS

There are far more papers published in the Middle East than one would think and they are usually seen in the hands of men in cafés. It is most unusual to see a village woman reading a paper. Though education schemes are making a difference, many women do not know how to read. Not many people are seen reading books. The Arabic alphabet and language are so complicated that the average intelligence finds it all it can do at school to master the bare essentials. Book publishing is not very profitable because all the author's friends expect free copies! Every kind of foreign newspaper and paperback can be found in towns and in the lounges of the international hotels. Censorship, in Syria and Iraq especially, sometimes acts to cut offending pages out of magazines, but this is sporadic.

("nashki"). The first went out of date in Medieval times.

Even people who cannot read think calligraphy is enormously important, as if there was something sacred in the act of writing. There was no such thing as a printing press in Islam till the eighteenth century — about a hundred years or more after Europe. Up till ten years ago, calligraphy with reed pens was taught as a separate subject, but it is now in with reading. The result is that the younger generation cannot write as well as the last.

The Khoran is, as always, a very important part of education and is often taught by a special teacher. The smaller children learn the shorter verses at the end.

The universities are overcrowded: in 1980 in Jordan there were 27,000 applicants for 3,000 places. The best pupils are sent abroad to study, but often find that, when they come back, there is no job for them. The law and medical professions are particularly overcrowded.

Calligraphy

Calligraphy is certainly the most typical and most common Muslim art form. Because Mohammed always stressed that he was nothing but the Messenger of God and not divine, the writing of "the Message" and the language in which "the Message" was written were of great importance. Writing was the only form of decoration and expression allowed — the Dome of the Rock, the first sacred building, has huge kufic writing in tiles round the drum.

There is no specific law in the Khoran that the living figure must not be represented, but Mohammed connected statues with pagan idols and from that might have followed the Islamic distrust of drawings of animals and people. Allah is the only true creator, and so he alone is able to instil the breath of life into his creations — images and pictures included. When Gertrude Bell was searching for archaeological remains in the

School in Syria.

desert, she was much handicapped by the fact that her Arab helpers found it very difficult to recognize a rock carving when they saw one. However, Muslim artists, when they were decorating the less holy places, did sometimes attempt to hide living creatures in the tracery of a tiled fountain or in a carpet. Constant contact with Greece and Persia through trade was bound to have its effect. Greek medical books, when translated, would not have made sense without the illustrations.

The Arabs and the Greeks

The Greek culture dawned upon the Arab consciousness with tremendous effect. It is a sobering thought that Greek civilization actually owes its survival to the Arabs. When the Arabs overran Syria in the first flush of their conquest, they found learned men in the Byzantine monasteries there, and were wise enough not only to leave them to get on with their studies but also actually to encourage them to translate all the Greek works of philosophy, mathematics, science, and other branches of learning into Syriac — which is the language from which Arabic is thought to have come. So the Arabs knew of decimal fractions two hundred years before Europe and the "zero" two hundred and fifty years before. (Without the "0", calculating is a very cumbersome business.)

The main fact is that a large part of Greek wisdom would never have reached the West but for the Arabs. During the Arab conquest a famous university was set up in Baghdad, whose main task was translating Greek works of science and philosophy from Greek into Arabic. The Arab translators became so interested in the teachings of Socrates and others that they began to question Islam. As a result, the university was closed and scholars took their books and fled to Cordoba which was then under the Moors. Many works were then translated into Spanish (from Arabic) and then into French and English.

A lot of English words beginning in "Al" or "Ad" are from the Arabic : for instance, "Admiral" comes from "Amir-el-Bahr". In those days "Amir" did not mean a "prince", as it does today, but a "commander". "Alchemy", a medieval form of chemistry, is easy to see. "Algebra" comes from the word "jabara", meaning "cut", and "el-jabr" means "the science of putting fractions together" — hence "algebra".

The Dicts and Sayings of the Philosophers was a collection of the sayings of philosophers (mostly Greek, including Socrates) compiled in the eleventh century in Arabic. It

was translated into English in 1477 and was one of the first books to be printed by Caxton in England. It was not the only book to have begun as an Arabic work. For instance, in the eighteenth century, the story of *The Arabian Nights* was a run-away best-seller. It ran through thirty editions in English. It was a collection of stories which were supposed to have been told by a slave called Shahrazzade to Harun-al-Rashid, a khalif in Baghdad. For some reason, he thought he had a perfect right to cut off her head if she did not amuse him. She told him stories for a thousand-and-one nights and then he had had enough and pardoned her. The book proved very popular in England in the eighteenth century, because of its exotic eastern flavour, at a time when reading was taking hold and people wanted something other than religious books. From *The Arabian Nights* came all the West's ideas of the "mysterious orient", with khalifs and djins and people in "dressing gowns", pointed shoes and huge turbans. The stories contained the spirit of adventure and paved the way to imaginative books like *Robinson Crusoe* and *Gulliver's Travels*.

The wheel came full circle and instead of Arabic books spreading to the West, Western books flowed into the Middle East. The problem in nearly all Middle East schools is that, for a long time past, all modern scientific works were written in English, French, German or Russian, so that higher teaching had to be in the hands of foreigners. Besides the complication of already having several local languages, pupils thus had to learn yet another language before they could go on to advanced studies. The isolated state of the countries of the Ottoman Empire before the First World War and the limited demand made translating into Arabic not worthwhile, and somehow the curiosity

An Arab finds it quicker on foot (Amman, Jordan).

which made the early Arabs devour Greek books was not enough when geography was in the way. When the Arab Empire no longer stretched round the Mediterranean, but had shrunk to one end of it, Arabs no longer came in daily contact with Greeks and other foreigners, and no longer felt the need to read their books or even to learn their language.

However, now, oil money allows printing presses to turn out foreign books locally. This is yet another process which is forcing the Arabs into a modern age — sometimes too fast for their comfort.

October

The Id el Adha

Id el Adha, the Feast of the Sacrifice, falls in October. The feast celebrates the faith in God of Abraham, which was so great that, when God asked him to sacrifice his only son, Isaac, he was prepared to do so. At the last moment God allowed him to substitute a ram.

The Id el Adha is the greatest feast of the Muslim year, lasting for three days. The main event is the sacrifice of a sheep. Every reasonably well-to-do family has one tethered in front of the door, ready to be slaughtered — sometimes by a special butcher — in the ritual way. The meat is then distributed to the poor, together with the money or alms which every good Muslim is instructed to donate at all times, and especially on feast days. Children are also given money on this day by their relatives and there is plenty to spend it on: fairs and donkey rides and carriage rides to the nearby parks. Paper windmills and balloons and plastic toys are sold in the streets. Bicycles can be hired which are perhaps more popular nowadays than the donkeys and carriages. They are decorated with little flags and streamers which make a pleasant festive rustle as the wheels spin round. The bicycles are also equipped with loud bells and horns, to be as noisy as possible and make people jump out of the way. This is all part of the fun. Everyone has new clothes.

During the three days of the feast friends and relations have to be visited. On the first day there is a race to get as many calls in as possible, so as to be able to sit at home for the rest of the time waiting for the doorbell to ring as the calls are returned. This can begin as early as 9 a.m. and continues till the last lights in the house are put out, at midnight, or later. Sweet fruit drinks are served and coffee and delicacies such as lumps of preserved fruit peel in syrup, on tiny silver filigree forks. After use these are dropped delicately into glasses of water handed round with the tray. The floor is usually awash with pistachio nut shells and sweet wrappings.

The Jews

Abraham is as important to Jews as to Muslims. He and Moses are considered the fathers of the Jewish race. The Jews acknowledge that it is only because of the miraculous birth of Isaac to Abraham's elderly wife,

Buying bread for Id el Adha.

Sarah, that Ishmael, Abraham's son by his concubine, Hagar, was superseded as the patriarch's natural heir whose descendants would inherit the Promised Land. Even then, the inheritance would have passed to Isaac's elder son, Esau, if his younger son, Jacob, had not stolen it by a trick. From early times the Ishmaelites appear in Jewish tradition as enemies, together with the Romans, and as rivals for the possession of the land of Israel.

To trace the history of the Jews: in Palestine, a few years after Mohammed's death in 632 A.D., the tribes which had come out of the Arabian desert, driven towards the sea by invaders from the East, acquired the name Hebrews, and one tribe or group of tribes called the Israelites claimed to be descended from Abraham's grandson, Jacob of Israel. By tradition, these Israelites went to Egypt, where they were badly treated by the Pharaohs until they found a leader in Moses, who managed to rescue most of his tribe and lead them back into Palestine. There they occupied most of the hilly country, because the coast was already taken up by the first-comers, the Phoenicians or Philistines living in Tyre and Sidon and Carthage on the African coast. We know these names today but very little about the people who lived there, except that they were great traders taking their boats all over the Mediterranean and even to Britain. The alphabet is their biggest contribution to world culture. They invented it to assist their trading activities.

The Israelites had quite a different claim to fame — it was they who first conceived the idea of one god, many hundreds of years before either Mohammed or Jesus had the idea. The Old Testament as we call it tells the story of the Jews, rather as the Khoran is about Muslims and the New Testament about Christianity. The first King of the Jews was David and afterwards came Solomon, who built the first temple at Jerusalem in 538 B.C. He made this town forever the centre of Jewish faith, even after it had been sacked by the Assyrian king Nebuchadnezzor, who removed all the Jews to Babylon, and even after it had been taken stone from stone by the Romans in a vain attempt to eliminate the Jews for good and all.

They seemed extraordinarily tough. After they had come back from Babylon, because the country was now under the Persian Cyrus, who was more benevolent, they rebuilt the temple and became a little island state. For the next three or four hundred years, until Pompey stormed Jerusalem in 63 B.C., they and their culture flourished. This is perhaps the period when their holy book of law, the Torah, took its final form and became the binding code of Jewish social life as well as of religion. It was also at this time that the Song of Solomon and some of the finest psalms were composed.

The Jews had a very hard time under the Romans who did not succeed in breaking them, though in the end many were killed

JEWISH FEAST DAYS

Jewish feast days are, for the most part, reminders of events in their long history and thanksgivings for the occasions on which God has been good to them. Like Muslim feasts, they are, of course, movable.

Passover or Pesach

This commemorates the exodus from Egypt where the Jews were badly treated. God appointed Moses as their leader, and led them out of captivity into the wilderness and eventually to a "land flowing with milk and honey" — i.e. Palestine. The family gather round a table for a meal which is taken standing up, as it remembers the last meal the Israelites took in Egypt before setting out. Unleavened bread is eaten in remembrance of the day when they had not had time to let it rise. The table is strewn with bitter herbs in memory of the hardships they endured. The head of the family recites the story of the exodus and it is the custom for the youngest child present to ask certain set questions about it, which receive ritual answers. Wine is drunk and, as the ten plagues which God inflicted on the Egyptians are recited, the drinkers put their fingers in their cups and shake a drop of wine onto the floor. This is to show that the joy of being liberated from the Egyptians is slightly lessened by the memory of the awful plagues their enemies had to endure.

The Day of Atonement or Yom Kippur

The centre of this day is a recitation of sins, in the synagogue. The congregation have to repeat after each one "we are guilty Oh Lord". Sometimes children find it hard to confess, because they hardly understand what sins like "adultery" mean.

The Jewish New Year or Succoth

On this day each family builds a booth of greenery in their garden or in any open space near their flat, to commemorate their life in the desert. In the Middle East the little green huts are often on flat roofs and look very pretty, decorated like Christmas trees with hanging fruits such as pomegranates and anything ornamental. It is a three-day feast. The religious part takes the form of "the Rejoicing of the Law", during which elderly men dance around the synagogue, holding up their skirts. It is a happy occasion.

The Feast of Lights or Hanukka

This is different from the other festivals, as it is not religious but a celebration of an important victory of the Jewish Maccabes against the Greeks a very long time ago. The centre of the feast is the branched candlestick or lamp. The lamps celebrate the time when, because of wars, the synagogue lamps were getting short of oil, but, by a miracle, they just managed to last until fresh supplies reached them.

and many more deported all over the world. The fortress of Massada near the Dead Sea which has just been excavated was one of the places where they held out desperately. Jesus was a Jew who lived in a Jewish land and founded his gospel on a basis of Jewish life and thought. When he was crucified by a Roman governor, who looked upon him as a trouble-maker, the accusation pinned up over his head was in all official languages spoken in the country — Greek, Latin and Hebrew — just as official notices during the British mandate of Palestine had to be in English, Arabic — and Hebrew.

When the Arabs conquered Palestine, the first thing they did, towards the end of the seventh century, was to erect the Dome of the Rock on the site of Solomon's temple, to demonstrate to the Jews that Islam was to replace Judaism from then on. Until very recently all unbelievers were barred from the Haram el Sherif, or the enclosure round the Dome of the Rock, as they still are from Mecca today. The Haram el Sherif, or Dome

of the Rock, is a glorious pavilion covering the living rock on top of a hill on which Jerusalem has always been rebuilt, no matter how many times destroyed. The hill is the kernel of the most holy place to three religions. By Muslim tradition, the rock bears the hoof-print of the winged horse "Burac", on which Mohammed is supposed to have journeyed by night. The original plan of the pavilion is as it was, but, unfortunately, the ancient and beautiful tiles have recently been replaced by dazzling new ones which have not the same charm. On the other hand, the split marble panelling, which has the effect of the patterns you make with ink blobs on paper, and the wonderful golden mosaics of the inside of the dome seem as they always were. Just outside the big building is a charming little building, sometimes called "The Treasury", an exact copy of the large Dome. It has not been restored at all and is exactly as it was in 691. Some people think it was a try-out of the Dome of the Rock.

During the time they were excluded from the site of the Temple of Solomon, the Jews had to be content with one part of the outer wall of the enclosure, which was just a fortuitous gap in the houses, in a narrow alley in Jerusalem old city. It came to be known as the "wailing wall", because the Jews went there to bewail the destruction of the temple. Today, the Arab houses have been cleared away and a large open space gives plenty of room for all the tourists who flock there from all over the world.

This month also remembers the October War in 1973, the third war between the Arabs and the Jews (see page 24). It is not to be wondered at that the Palestine Royal Commission of 1936, sent out to make one of the earliest of countless attempts at peace, was surprised at the wideness of the gulf and the near impossibility of bridging it. "Two nations warring in the bosom of a single state," they called it — and that country not much larger than Wales. "Such a conflict in a land consecrated to three world religions . . . is tragic enough in itself, but the more tragic . . . because it is fundamentally a conflict of right with right . . . no other problem of our time is rooted so deeply in the past."

November

Muharram, the first month of the Muslim year, is now. The first ten days are considered holy, especially Yom el Ashura, meaning the Tenth Day. This is not a public holiday, but in the mosque the first meeting of Adam and Eve after they had left Paradise is remembered, and also God's forgiveness. A legend has it that the black stone in the sacred Ka'aba at Mecca was God's consola- tion to Adam for being deprived of the Garden of Eden. Popular belief puts this Paradise at various places in the Middle East; Qurna, in Iraq, where the Euphrates and the Tigris meet to form the Shatt el Arab, is high on the list.

The Jewish fast of Yom Kippur, the Day of Atonement, falls here too. When Islam first began, the Muslims used to fast on this

day too, until Mohammed moved the fast to another part of the year and made it a whole month — Ramadan.

Marsh Arab house.

Ur-of-the-Chaldees

This month of Muharram also commemorates the ending of Noah's flood — another sign of God's relenting. This takes us to Iraq as well, because in the early 1930s Sir Leonard Woolley, the British archaeologist, thought he had discovered "The Flood" during his excavations at Ur-of-the-Chaldees in southern Iraq. He was excited at finding two metres of pure alluvium laid by flood over the ruins of the ancient town. But modern archaeologists have found many more signs of flooding all over the south of the country and all through history to the present time. Until recently the two rivers regularly overflowed each spring and early summer, causing much devastation.

The most dramatic part of Woolley's work at Ur was the excavation of the Royal Tombs and the death pit, with its grim evidence of a funeral ritual as has not been discovered in this form anywhere else in the Middle East. When the king died, all his family and all his court — musicians with their harps, soldiers with their weapons and court ladies in gorgeous clothes, including wreaths of gold-leaf — willingly followed their master into the pits, where they were drugged into a painless death. This "never fails to leave an unforgettable feeling of horror mingled with wonder and admiration". In his graphic description, Woolley brings it all vividly into our imagination with a picture of one court lady "late for her own funeral", whose gold hair ribbon was discovered still folded up in her pocket as if she had not had time to put it on. The dresses and many other finds painstakingly restored by Woolley and his wife can be seen in the British Museum.

Iraq

Iraq means in Arabic "cliff". To the west, where the desert fades into Syria and Jordan, there are ghostly outlines of cliffs marking a very ancient seashore. This faint shoreline with the actual shore of the Shatt el Arab forms the boundary of a vast marshland which is a living museum. On the thousands of small islands formed by matted reed beds are still to be seen the plaited reed houses, as depicted on ancient Sumerian reliefs. The inhabitants paddle slender boats with upturned prows like Venetian gondolas — exact replicas of the ones Sir Leonard Woolley dug up at Ur-of-the-Chaldees. The modern "Marsh Arabs" have faces in which you can find traces of all the different peoples who have passed that shortest way from India and the Far East to the Mediterranean and Europe.

The Western world dreams of Baghdad, the capital of Iraq, as a romantic city, the scene of many of the Arabian Nights stories. Harun-al-Rashid, who ruled there in the eighth century A.D., is a name which has resounded round the world, symbolizing all that is rich and hardly imaginable. But once the glory of the khalifs had faded, Baghdad and Iraq became a stagnant outpost, too far

Marsh Arab woman in a village north of Basra.

away to be administered properly by the Ottomans who ruled the other Middle East countries for four hundred years. What Hulagu the Mongol, grandson of Ghenghis Khan, and Tamurlain had not achieved in destruction was completed by gradual decline and neglect. Between the two world wars the British looked after Iraq with, for a time, Gertrude Bell as Oriental Secretary. After the Second World War the Arab nationalism which worked in other countries of the Middle East swept away the king and his court who were considered too pro-British, and again it was army-trained men who took over.

The frontier lines which divide Iraq from its neighbours are artificial lines drawn in the desert. They are unusual, because between Iraq, Kuwait, Saudi Arabia and Jordan a neutral zone is vital to facilitate the migration of pastoral nomads who cover great distances each year in search of pasture for animals and who move regularly between several countries. Closing the frontiers could be a matter of life and death to them.

A griffin-like creature moulded in the bricks, Babylon.

In 1975 a big new oil field was discovered in Iraq, which makes it the second largest Middle East oil producer. The oil money has been used for irrigation and flood control schemes.

Visiting Iraq

From May to October inclusive it is probably too hot for visiting the wonders. The temperature can be 125° and it is very humid.

Travellers are often disappointed when they first find themselves in Baghdad, the city of Harun-al-Rashid and the Arabian Nights. There is not much left of the Hanging Gardens of Babylon, once one of the Seven Wonders of the World. Mud brick and most especially unbaked mud brick does not leave impressive ruins. As firewood was expensive, only gods' houses were built of burnt brick, like the great "ziggurats" whose ruins today look like artificial mountains in the flat land. Sometimes the burnt bricks were held together with bitumen and that had to be brought hundreds of miles from a bitumen lake in Armenia.

Travellers are seldom disappointed in Ctesiphon, which experts say is the widest single-span vault of un-reinforced brickwork in the world. It is about 23 metres wide and 33 metres high. Standing directly under it, and gazing at the single course of bricks arching against the deep blue sky, you wonder why it does not fall, but each brick leans into the next so comfortably that it has remained there for well over a thousand years. The banqueting hall was built by the Parthians, a mysterious horseback people from inner Mongolia, who are supposed to have invented trousers — or riding breeches! During the Arab conquest many old buildings were used as mosques and this marvellous super-tent in the middle of the desert was greeted by the Bedouin armies with rapture. But they were soon moved to more austere barracks and instructions were given that the paintings then covering the walls were not to be damaged. They have long since disappeared. Mohammed himself, in his aesthetic way, 'did not approve of rich buildings to worship in — he is supposed to have said that "Nothing so much wastes the substance of a believer as architecture."

Pilgrimage to Mecca

The end of October or the beginning of November sees the five-day pilgrimage to Mecca or Id el Kubir. Although this is the best time to go to Mecca, as it was sanctified by Mohammed's visit, in modern times any part of the year is permitted. Pilgrimage outside of the special pilgrimage time is called "omrah" or "good for the soul".

Each day in the present time a quarter of the world's population turns five times in prayer towards the city of Mecca, where Mohammed was born and which is the spiritual home of Islam. They turn towards the Ka'aba which is a building originally put up as a pagan temple incorporating a black stone. The stone is the most sacred thing in existence to the Muslims, because it was kissed by Mohammed.

Though he had been born in the city, the Prophet made only one visit to the Ka'aba

The sixteenth-century Kadimain Shrine in Baghdad. Entry is forbidden to non-Muslims.

just before his death, to demonstrate that it had been purified and purged of paganism. Whatever Mohammed did on this only visit became law. Some of the pagan practices persist into Islamic rites, such as picking up forty-nine stones and throwing them at a certain pillar to cast out evil spirits or the devil, and going round the Ka'aba seven times. Mohammed did this and so it was no longer a pagan rite. Mohammed's visit took place in the month of Dhu al Hijja, as was usual in pagan times, and so from then on that was the month for pilgrimage.

The Khoran commands that a Muslim shall make the pilgrimage at least once in a lifetime if at all possible. This journey is called the "Hajj" and the men or women who do it are from then on called "Hajji". No non-Muslim will ever witness this vast gathering of human beings from all over the world. But recently, for the first time, Muslim photographers have been allowed, so that it is easier to form a picture of the "human beehive", as one traveller has called it.

Many of the pilgrims come from within Saudi Arabia and it is also through Jeddah

65

that foreign pilgrims arrive, by sea and air, at the rate of over 50,000 travellers a day — the equivalent of two Boeing 747s every three minutes. The number of Muslims in the world today is over 1,000 million and it is becoming easier in every way for them to travel to Mecca. Besides the facilities of air travel which make it generally easier to get there, the Saudi Arabians have now waived some of the costs such as an entry due and obligatory donations which used to be levied for the upkeep of the holy places. The Saudis do not actually pay the fares of all the pilgrims, but sometimes establish funds for the needy. For example, if a Sheikh goes to Cairo, he will leave a sum of money there for poor would-be pilgrims. The Saudi Arabians have also built a huge Madinat al Hujaj (pilgrims' city) instead of the tent city where pilgrims used to live.

Passports are carefully examined by police, in case an "unbeliever" should try to slip in, and everything is arranged by the "mutawwif" — "those who guide others in the "tawaf" (the circling of the Ka'aba)". They are identified by a special badge and act rather like travel agents. Some families use the same ones for generations.

Pilgrims on their way to Mecca, boarding a special Haj ship in Karachi, Pakistan.

The pilgrim takes leave of his family and friends in a ceremony at which special hymns are sung with the "mushayin" or "those from whom leave is taken". Before he joins the "human whirlpool" round the Ka'aba, he must enter into a state of "ihram" or grace. This means performing the "ghusl" or major ablution, cutting hair and trimming nails for the last time before he returns home. No perfume must be used and all clothes must be seamless. He is only allowed to wear two white sheets or towels, one round his body and the other draped over his shoulders, held on by a seamless belt. His sandals must be without stitching. He must not take the life of any living thing, not the smallest fly. He must refrain from sex. It is not obligatory for women to go to Mecca, but many of them do and they mix freely with the men. They wear their normal clothes, white if possible. They are barred if they are menstruating. One pilgrim described seeing an old Bedouin woman dancing in the mosque.

The Ka'aba is draped in a black cloth called the "kisweh", which is richly embroidered round the edges in gold. According to worshippers, the Ka'aba seems to float on the shoulders of the dense throng that eddies round it, struggling to get as near as possible. Often the men link arms to protect women or old men too weak to fend for

themselves. Everyone has brought a prayer mat but there is hardly room to kneel. It seems to be a real feat of endurance to get round the seven statutory times.

Prayers are led by the Imam through microphones. Every day there are prayers for the dead. There are, on average, about a hundred-and-fifty deaths a day, since many pilgrims are old and ill.

The tomb of the Prophet at Medina, a nearby town, is visited by most pilgrims, but this is not obligatory. Water from the sacred fountain of Zem Zem is sold in bottles and flasks which are taken home. The water is still as abundant as in the old days, though it now runs more hygienically through taps and pipes, instead of spurting out in a fountain.

Pilgrims often speak of the wonderful feeling of peace and one-ness with the world which they feel during and after the journey. One describes how the simple act of sharing a small prayer mat crystallizes this feeling. Pilgrims put up with petty worries more than they would ever do normally. The perfect pilgrim in the past was instructed to "smile at your donkey or camel driver, keep on good terms with him throughout the journey, listen politely to his chatter". The modern equivalent to camel and donkey drivers are the drivers of the thousands of cars, lorries and buses which carry the pilgrims from the air and sea ports to Mecca. They are ceaselessly being offered bribes to take short cuts and often the overloaded cars have to be pulled out of ditches by ever-watchful police. But it is all taken cheerfully — or so it is said.

In medieval times the women were only allowed to visit the Ka'aba on a Thursday (they had a special paved path for making the walk seven times round it). It was therefore thought necessary to wash down the whole building and courtyard on Thursday evening, because the women took their small children in with them, who were not "trained".

In December 1979 a group of fanatics tried to take over the Great Mosque in Mecca. A well-known saying, attributed to the Prophet Mohammed, was that at the beginning of every century (calculated by the Hijjra calendar) a messenger would appear bearing his name and would be recognized by the people at the Great Mosque at Mecca. He would usher in a new golden age. 1979 was the beginning of the fourteenth century, according to the Hijjra calendar. As the new century approached, there was an air of expectancy among the pious. A "messenger" was soon found to fit the description and plans were made to show him to the people in the mosque.

The preparations had a military precision. The new "followers" stored arms and supplies in the cellars beneath the mosque. In the old days, when travelling was much more difficult than it is today, many pilgrims stayed behind after the ceremonies were over, either because they were too ill to move, or because they had no money for the return journey. In the cellars they could find refuge. In these days of air travel they no longer need to do this.

When the great day came, the "Messenger" and his followers entered the mosque from underground passages. He got hold of the microphone, used by the preacher. "Your attention oh Muslims"! he said. "God is great. The Messenger has appeared. Remember the words of the Prophet, now is the time! This is the man!" But the people did not respond. The guards moved in and the shooting started. King Khaled of Saudi Arabia and his government were taken completely by surprise; in the holiest place in the Islamic world it was unthinkable to use tanks to break open doors of the mosque. The dilemma lasted for fifteen days. In the end, a secret underground passage was found which led close to the rebels. Sensitive listening devices helped spy on them. Then the whole area was surrounded with specially trained commandos. The "followers" were soon flushed out with the help of gas, many of them killed and the crisis was over.

December

This month is considered unlucky by the Muslims, because it is furthest away from the holy month of Ramadan, and pilgrimage to Mecca was sometimes forbidden in this period.

Christmas and Bethlehem

In what Christians call the Holy Land, Bethlehem, the place where Jesus Christ was born, is crowded with pilgrims. There are so many kinds of Christians wanting to celebrate Christmas in what is reputed to be the site of the manger that there has to be a rota. The Armenians, who celebrate the birth of Christ on 6 January, have to wait their turn at the manger until the 19 January.

Though, once you are inside, the Church of the Nativity looks like an ordinary church, from the outside it looks more like a fortress with a blank wall and a very small door which, it is said, was kept small so that the Saracens could not ride their horses through. In this country, where three religions are constantly at war, holy places often look embattled. The manger, which a traveller at the beginning of this century described as "like a modern fireplace without a grate", is not actually visible. The most striking thing is a brass star set into a white marble floor, rather like a brass in an English church. The whole effect is of a rich cave hung with banners and lit with rich lamps. The very brass nails which hold the star to the marble are each owned and fought over by some religious sect jealously guarding its tiny foothold in Bethlehem. (For centuries the guardians of some of the Christian holy places have been Muslim — to keep the peace between the different sects of Christians.)

A ceremony in this little manger space is even more claustrophobic than in the Church of the Holy Sepulchre, with incense

The Church of the Nativity, Bethlehem.

68

JESUS CHRIST AND CHRISTIANS
IN THE MIDDLE EAST; THE BIBLE

Jesus did not write any books and what he said was not taken down by his contemporaries as was the case with Mohammed. The authenticated facts about his life are few. The most certain is that he was crucified in about A.D. 28-30. His followers claimed that he had risen from the dead. Those who held this belief gradually broke away from the mainstream of Jewish religion and became known as "Christians", because of their belief that Jesus was the "Christ" — a Greek word which is the equivalent of the Hebrew word "Messiah", meaning the "anointed one". The coming of this Messiah had long been expected by the Jews. There are enough references to the death of Jesus in Roman and Greek writings to know that he really did exist. The rest of the events before, during and after his life are open to conjecture.

The Bible is a collection of documents regarded by the Christians and the Jews as embodying the word of God. It is divided into the Old Testament, the Apocrypha, and the New Testament. The Old Testament consists of those books recognized by Jews — chiefly the Law (like the Khoran) and the writings of the Prophets. The Christians too recognized the Old Testament and added to it the New Testament which records the life, death and resurrection of Jesus, and also the teachings of early Christian preachers. The Apocrypha is regarded as not so authentic as the Old and New Testaments.

Religious division is still very strong in the Middle East and for many people it replaces division by nationality. Christianity in the Middle East has many branches because of the development of religious feeling during and after the end of the Roman Empire. There arose the Greek Orthodox Church and the Roman Catholic Church (called the Latin Church in the Middle East). The Nestorians were once very widespread; they did most of the translating of the Greek philosophers and scientists. Then there are the Armenians (or Gregorians) and the Maronites. These are the chief Christian groups. In the nineteenth century, Protestant missionaries from many European countries added to the tapestry, but they did not make many converts. As might be expected, the greatest number of Christians of all kinds live in Israel and Jordan, as near as possible to the Holy Places.

and smoking candles and endless chanting. A traveller described a Christmas ceremony:

the voices coming out of the cave sounded hollow and unnatural. I felt I was witnessing the ritual of a ghostly sabbath. Seen through the doorway at the foot of the stair this little lamp-lit company of kneeling men in the attitude of the adoring Magi in their medieval dress with their tapers and missals formed a scene out of the days of the Middle Ages. The light which lit the faces of the monks came from unseen lamps and might have poured through an opening in the cave from the setting sun of five centuries ago. (From *The Land that was Desolate* by Sir F. Treves, Bt, 1912)

Books for Further Reading

The Arabs, Peter Mansfield, Penguin Books
The History of the Crusades, Steven Runciman, Penguin Books, three vols.
The Middle East and North Africa, Europa Publications (Revised yearly; various experts. Very up-to-date)
Mirror to Damascus, Colin Thubron, Heinemann (1967)
Mohammed, Maxime Rodinson, Penguin Books
The Spread of Islam, Michael Rogers, Elsevie-Phaidon
The World of Islam, various authors, Thames and Hudson (well-illustrated)

Index